W9-BSH-793

"In *The Measure of a Man* my friend and mentor, Dr. Gene Getz, has laid a foundation for biblical manhood that any male can use to build the superstructure of a solid life. It is past time for men to aspire to God's definition of who we are to be rather then the flawed definitions of our contemporary culture. This book will enable you to do just that."

—**Tony Evans**, president, The Urban Alternative;
senior pastor, Oak Cliff Bible Fellowship

"Before God makes the ministry, He measures and makes the man. Gene Getz has been God's tool for making many a man during this generation. His book has shaped me professionally and his friendship has marked me personally. I am so happy to see this classic book in a new, impactful edition. "

—**Dr. James MacDonald**, senior pastor, Harvest Bible Chapel;
author, *Act Like Men* and *Vertical Church*

"It strikes me that it would take either a colossal ego or deep humility to write a book subtitled 'Twenty Attributes of a Godly Man.' For nearly fifty years, Gene Getz has been my respected mentor, stellar example, treasured colleague, and beloved friend. Humility has always been his hallmark."

—**Jerry B. Jenkins**, novelist and biographer,
The Jerry Jenkins Writers Guild

"*The Measure of a Man* is a great reference work for any man seeking the definition of biblical masculinity. It has helped me in my faith journey and I have passed it along to my son and other young men to help guide them in theirs."

—**Chad Hennings**, three-time Super Bowl Champion;
founder, Wingmen Ministries

"I have read and used the book *The Measure of a Man* to help train many church leaders . . . the book truly transcends culture. I'm excited with this new edition, for it has made the reading and study of it easier for churches, groups, and individuals. . . . This book, as I know, has been very effective in helping men to become spiritual leaders at home and in the church; for this reason it has never gone out of print. It has been translated into many languages, including Hausa here in Nigeria, to motivate men to live a more Christlike life. I therefore highly recommend this book to every man, father, and husband; fellowship groups; and Christian organizations, for it will not only change your life but that of your church and organization."

—**Dr. Musa Asake**, National General Secretary, Christian
Association of Nigeria (CAN), Abuja, Nigeria

"Occasionally a book stands out among the mass of published literature as a 'must read' and, in fact, a book that you know you will want to read again. Such is the case with *The Measure of a Man*. This book has had a global, transformational impact over the last few decades, and thankfully my friend Gene Getz has revisited the text and brought it up to speed for a new generation. If somehow you missed this book before, now is the time to pick it up and open your heart and mind to its powerfully relevant message."

—Joseph M. Stowell, president, Cornerstone University, Grand Rapids, Michigan

"In our cultural penchant for quick results, quantitative metrics trump qualitative measures for longer-term growth toward spiritual health. *The Measure of a Man* explores key indices of an applied spiritual process, stimulating self-examination, then self-management, as men serve as leaders of families, businesses, and ministries. As always, Gene Getz addresses biblical claims which transcend culture, age, economics, and race, with pastoral care. Since he himself has lived out the spiritual process over the decades, his practical depth is credibly presented to all men who wish to live in a godly way in an ungodly age which disparages, and even degrades, their gender."

—Ramesh Richard, ThD, PhD, president, Ramesh Richard Evangelism and Church Health; professor, Global Theological Engagement and Pastoral Ministries, Dallas Theological Seminary

"When I was a young coach and husband, my marriage ended in divorce. That's when a Christian friend and mentor recommended *The Measure of a Man*. These principles changed my life. I remarried my wife and have been happily married for 47 years. It also allowed me to model character to my coaches and players for 30 years. When I became a head coach and later an administrator, these same principles guided my hiring and evaluations."

—Coach Tommy Cox, Texas High School Coaches Association

"I was first exposed to *The Measure of a Man* as a Bible college student. I was saved out of a non-Christian family and reading this book transformed my life. Today—years later—I'm using it to equip the men in my church with the same life-changing results."

—Edward M. Trinkle, lead pastor, Canyon Creek Church

THE
MEASURE
OF A
MAN

TWENTY ATTRIBUTES OF A
GODLY MAN

GENE A. GETZ

Revell

a division of Baker Publishing Group
Grand Rapids, Michigan

© 1974, 2004, 2016 by Gene A. Getz

Published by Revell
a division of Baker Publishing Group
P.O. Box 6287, Grand Rapids, MI 49516-6287
www.revellbooks.com

Printed in the United States of America

All rights reserved. No part of this publication may be reproduced, stored in a retrieval system, or transmitted in any form or by any means—for example, electronic, photocopy, recording—without the prior written permission of the publisher. The only exception is brief quotations in printed reviews.

Library of Congress Cataloging-in-Publication Data
Names: Getz, Gene A., author.
Title: The measure of a man : twenty attributes of a godly man / Gene A. Getz.
Description: Grand Rapids : Revell, [2016]. | Includes bibliographical references.
Identifiers: LCCN 2016019453 | ISBN 9780800722388 (pbk.)
Subjects: LCSH: Christian men—Religious life.
Classification: LCC BV4843 .G47 2016 | DDC 248.8/42—dc23
LC record available at https://lccn.loc.gov/2016019453

Unless otherwise indicated, Scripture quotations are from the New American Standard Bible®, copyright © 1960, 1962, 1963, 1968, 1971, 1972, 1973, 1975, 1977, 1995 by The Lockman Foundation. Used by permission. (www.Lockman.org)

Scripture quotations labeled AMP are from the Amplified® Bible, copyright © 1954, 1958, 1962, 1964, 1965, 1987 by The Lockman Foundation. Used by permission. (www.Lockman.org)

Scripture quotations labeled ASV are from the American Standard Version of the Bible.

Scripture quotations labeled KJV are from the King James Version of the Bible.

Scripture quotations labeled NIV are from the Holy Bible, New International Version®. NIV®. Copyright © 1973, 1978, 1984, 2011 by Biblica, Inc.™ Used by permission of Zondervan. All rights reserved worldwide. www.zondervan.com

The author has added emphasis to Scripture by italicizing words and phrases.

20   21   22   23   8   7   6

In keeping with biblical principles of creation stewardship, Baker Publishing Group advocates the responsible use of our natural resources. As a member of the Green Press Initiative, our company uses recycled paper when possible. The text paper of this book is composed in part of post-consumer waste.

First, I'd like to dedicate this edition of *The Measure of a Man* to my son, Kenton, and my five grandsons: Kyle, Corban, Caleb, Carter, and Cooper!

Second, this book is dedicated to all the men who have told me over the years how *The Measure of a Man* has changed their lives! Thank you!

Now to Him who is able to do far more abundantly beyond all that we ask or think, according to the power that works within us, to Him be the glory in the church and in Christ Jesus to all generations forever and ever. Amen.

Ephesians 3:20–21

Table of Contents

Foreword

As an excited young seminary student, I first found my way to Fellowship Bible Church in the fall of 1976. The church had been launched only four years prior by Dr. Gene Getz as a bold experiment to put into practice what he had been teaching in the classroom. I often sat on a cushion in the aisle due to the size of the crowds, but the inconvenience of the seating never dulled the clear, practical teaching which I absorbed like a sponge.

Through my seminary years I remained involved in the ministry of Gene's church and chose to be part of the group to plant a new church in the Park Cities. It would be an understatement to say Gene had a significant role in my spiritual formation as a believer, and later, as a Christian leader. When I became the president of the Moody Bible Institute in 2009, it was a heartfelt joy to see Gene's warm, smiling face on the Board of Trustees. Even though he has retired from our board, he remains a dear friend, prayer partner, and wise counselor.

I relate that history because I believe this book, *The Measure of a Man*, captures the essence of Gene's ministry more than any of his dozens of other publications. First printed in 1974, this book has remained in print over the past forty years because it provides thoroughly biblical but intensely practical help for Christian men who are striving to press forward in their spiritual maturity. Walking carefully through the Pauline qualifications for elders found in 1 Timothy 3 and Titus 1, it provides a path to follow for those who not only aspire to be leaders in their local church, but also want to be better husbands, fathers, and friends. My original copy, several decades old, is dog-eared from the many times I have referred to it.

This edition is especially valuable, for it not only contains the same rich (but updated) content from previous editions but it also has embedded QR codes. A quick flick of your smartphone and you can view a video of Gene teaching on the principle found in the text. The use of this technology will only increase the impact of this book.

If you have studied this book in the past, I urge you to revisit it like an old friend. If this is your first time to pick it up, I assure you that you are in for a treat. Like I did forty years ago, grab a cushion and enjoy!

J. Paul Nyquist, PhD
President, Moody Bible Institute

A Word from the Author

Welcome to a multimedia edition of *The Measure of a Man*. In this new edition, I've added QR codes—one at the beginning of each chapter and one at the end. In fact, I've also included two different codes in the Introduction, which will give you some background information and help you launch into this study.

You can scan these QR codes with your smartphone or tablet and access video teaching. In the chapter opening videos, I'll introduce you to the content in each chapter. These brief presentations are designed to prepare your mind and heart before you read.

The closing videos at the end of each chapter are designed to facilitate group discussion and application. These encouraging videos supplement the book material entitled "Thinking and Growing Together."

I first used these helpful QR codes in the *Life Essentials Study Bible*—the first ever multimedia study Bible. This Bible includes 1,500 "Principles to Live By" with 1,500 QR codes embedded with each principle, enabling the reader to access 1,500 video teaching presentations.

There are many free QR readers available for smartphones and tablets. Check your own device. It may have one already installed.

Gene A. Getz

Introduction

Growing Together

Five Super Bowls Later!

One day I received a call from D. D. Lewis, former linebacker with the Dallas Cowboys. "I'm in trouble," D. D. said, "and I need help! Will you help me?"

A Video Welcome from Gene

renewal.tv/mmi

D. D.'s voice sounded desperate. "Sure," I replied. "Let's meet Thursday morning."

While playing with the Cowboys, D. D. attended the church I pastored. After participating in five Super Bowls under Coach Tom Landry, he eventually retired and went into business. At some point, he had stopped attending church and I had lost contact with him.

Unfortunately, things didn't go well for D. D. He experienced two business failures and eventually went through a painful divorce that also left him alienated from his children. Although he was a professing Christian, his life had deteriorated. Addictive actions controlled his life.

As we met that Thursday morning, this man who had once been so powerful on the football field poured out his sad story. He knew he needed spiritual help and more accountability.

Getting Back on Track

As I sat with D. D. that day, I saw the desperation in his eyes. "I'll help you," I replied. "Let's meet once a week for breakfast, and then work through a book I wrote called *The Measure of a Man.*" D. D. was grateful. He committed to read a chapter each week, and then we would meet to talk, discuss, and pray.

"You'll need to be honest with me," I said. "No secrets. If you fail in some area of your life, you'll need to admit it up front."

Again, D. D. agreed and together we worked through the chapters in this book. Later, he wrote me:

> Meeting with you and going through your book, *The Measure of a Man*, helped usher me back into renewed relationships with the family of God. This study showed me that God *does* have a design and standard for godly men to follow. With your loving encouragement, I have been able to see that God loves me in spite of my past behavior (Titus 3:3–7), and that my journey toward maturity is a process and not an overnight quick-fix emotional sensation.
>
> Our time together fostered in me a real thirst for God's Word. It has sustained me through some rough periods and trials. I have found out that most men have the same problems over the years, and that healing begins when we share ourselves with other godly men.

A Dynamic Bible Study

As D. D. and I sat week after week, working through *The Measure of a Man*, my thoughts went back to a dynamic Bible study I had with a group of men in Dallas. We met to discover from Scripture and from each other how we could become better husbands, better fathers, better Christians—in short, more mature men of God.

In the fall of 1972, I had just helped plant the first Fellowship Bible Church. I invited our men to join me in an early morning Bible study. As a basis for our study, I suggested Paul's maturity profiles in his letters to Timothy and Titus (1 Tim. 3:1–7; Titus 1:5–9).

To launch our time together, I led the group to discuss from Scripture what Paul meant by being "above reproach"—the first quality he outlined in both letters. And then in the light of our biblical insights, we discussed how to develop this quality in our lives.

At the end of this introductory session, I asked for volunteers to lead our next studies. At that point—even though they looked to me as their lead pastor—I became a learner with all of these men. And what happened from week to week was a dynamic and exciting experience—so much so I began to carefully journal what we were learning from each other.

About six weeks into this study, Bill Grieg, Jr., who was then President of Gospel Light Publications, stopped by my office. He had heard about what was happening at Fellowship Bible Church. We had created some new and fresh forms for teaching, worship, fellowship, and outreach and were growing rapidly. Anxious to know more about our ministry, Bill asked for some specifics. In essence, what was happening?

Excited about our men's study, I shared what I had been journaling. Captivated by my notes, Bill said, "Gene, I want this as a book! Will you use these qualities to write a book on maturity?"

I was surprised—yet challenged. In fact, at that moment, Bill handed me a contract—any writer's dream. The end result is the book you're reading—*The Measure of a Man*!

Going Deeper

As I met with D. D. Lewis week after week, I was reproducing one-on-one what I had done with the original group of men several years before. The difference, of course, is that D. D. and I had the book in hand—which formed a foundation to guide us to even greater depths of understanding and application.

Little did I realize when I first wrote this book that God was going to continue to use it in a variety of ways for many years to come—in small group studies, one-on-one mentoring, and discipling, just as I used it with D. D. Lewis as a means to help him forget what was behind and to press forward to what was ahead—to become more and more a man after God's own heart (Phil. 3:12–14).

Building Up One Another

In describing the church and how it is to function, the apostle Paul used a metaphor of the human body. His point was this: Just as our physical bodies have many members and all of these body parts have unique functions, "so we, who are many, are one body in Christ, and individually members of one another" (Rom. 12:4–5). And, as Paul later wrote to the Ephesians, we are all to "attain to the unity of the faith, and of the knowledge of the Son of God, to a *mature man*, to the *measure of the stature which belongs to the fullness of Christ*" (Eph. 4:13).

Paul then went on to make it clear that this will not happen as God intended unless "every joint supplies, according to the proper working of each individual part." Then and only then the body of Christ will grow and mature in love (Eph. 4:16).

Thinking and Growing Together

My prayer is that you will apply Paul's instructions in a specific way by joining with other men for this study. You may have already joined a group. If so, would you make a commitment to the Lord and the other men that you will do all you can to read the chapters in *The Measure of a Man* and then participate in the application discussions outlined at the end of each chapter?

A Video Challenge from Gene

renewal.tv/mmr

If you've not been invited to be a part of a group, consider starting your own. Invite other men to join you in this study. Or, you

16

might already have an accountability partner. If so, suggest that the two of you use this study as you meet regularly—preferably week to week.

Or, here's another suggestion. Do you know someone you could mentor and disciple—someone you can build your own life into? Perhaps this is your son. Or remember, there are many men around you who have not had a good father figure in their lives. By using *The Measure of a Man*, you can be that father figure.

Set a Goal

As a result of this chapter, write out a goal you would like to achieve in your own life—and in the lives of others:

Eliminate fear of mens doing and establish a closer "fear" of God (which is not "fear" but a relationship of honesty + integrity with the Almighty, so that we become closer friends and family in heirship and sonship)

Pray for One Another

Once each man has written out a goal, allow time to share the goals with others and to pray for each other.

Note: No one in the group should feel forced to share or pray. On the other hand, no one should be excluded from participating.

1

Becoming a Faithful Man

Insights from the Workaday World

I had a fascinating experience one day when I was conducting a "Measure of a Man Seminar" in Chicago. I was talking about the profile of maturity that Paul outlined in his letters to Timothy and Titus. Two men sitting near the front row were obviously very intrigued! While I was speaking, they actually gave me positive feedback—not only with body language, but also with words such as: "That's right, Gene"; "That's true"; "That's a good point."

A Personal Message from Gene

renewal.tv/mm1i

During the coffee break, I went over and sat at their table. They were both in upper management in a large steel mill in Gary, Indiana. Spiritually, they were both new Christians. As we chatted, one of them said, "Gene, this is outstanding material."

The other man agreed, and then added—"Yeah, I've heard of Timothy before, but this Titus guy, I've *never* heard of him."

At that moment, I knew I was relating to men who were not only new believers in Jesus Christ, but men who knew very little about the Bible. However, they were not new to the field of management.

During our conversation they made an observation I'll never forget. "You know," they said, "this is the first time we've heard this list of qualifications from the Bible. But we've learned from experience in hiring people for middle-management positions that these are the kind of employees we're looking for." In essence, they went on to say they wanted employees who have a good reputation. If men were cheating on their wives or sleeping around, chances were they would also cheat on the company. They didn't want men who had all kinds of domestic problems. If they couldn't handle their own families, how in the world were they going to handle other employees?

How do we recognize a "man of God"? What does he look like?

To my surprise, these two men went on to outline more characteristics that correlated with Paul's maturity profile. Because of this seminar experience, they were learning that what they had gained from experience closely paralleled a biblical profile.

Needless to say, I was intrigued and fascinated. We had been looking at qualities of maturity inspired by the Holy Spirit and outlined by Paul nearly 2,000 years ago. And here were two men who were new Christians, men who knew little about the Bible—but they had learned from experience that this biblical profile is pragmatic and essential in selecting mature people who will serve in responsible positions.

Timothy in Ephesus

When Paul wrote his second letter to Timothy, he referred to a "man of God" who is "equipped for every good work" (2 Tim. 3:17). This raises an important question. How do we recognize this kind of man? What does he look like?

These are not new questions. They were going through Timothy's mind when Paul left him in Ephesus to establish the church.

He had to deal with men who wanted to be spiritual leaders but in some cases were very immature. They weren't qualified. Some were driven by a desire to have power over others.

On the other hand, some were sincere and Paul commended them for aspiring to serve in a leadership role. But he cautioned Timothy to make sure that each man who wanted to serve had reached a certain level of maturity and reflected "the stature which belongs to the fullness of Christ" (Eph. 4:13; 1 Tim. 3:1–7).

Titus in Crete

Titus faced the same challenge. Paul had left him in Crete to appoint spiritual leaders in towns where they had established churches (see Titus 1:5). Again, Paul cautioned Titus to make sure that these men measured up to certain Christ-like qualities.

Apparently, Titus faced problems in Crete that were more difficult to resolve than those Timothy faced in Ephesus. Men who claimed to be Christ-followers had emerged and were destroying "whole families, teaching things they should not *teach* for the sake of sordid gain" (v. 11). Their primary motives were materialistic. Titus faced the awesome task of not only discovering leaders and training them to be godly but also of silencing those who were "empty talkers and deceivers" (v. 10).

Paul's Maturity Profile

Two paragraphs in Paul's letters to Timothy and Titus give us this powerful profile for testing maturity levels in Christ, both personally and in others (see 1 Tim. 3:1–7; Titus 1:5–10). The following list depicts nineteen spiritual qualifications compiled from both letters with a succinct definition:

- Above reproach (a man of good reputation)
- The husband of one wife (morally pure)

- Temperate (balanced in words and actions) — *hot words → cold action*
- Prudent (wise and humble) — *Not so humble*
- Respectable (good role model) — *9 or so to*
- Hospitable (unselfish and generous) — *selfish → cheap*
- Able to teach (communicates sensitively in a nonthreatening and nondefensive manner) — *2. maybe*
- Not addicted to wine (not addicted to substances) — *w/ meal?*
- Not self-willed (not self-centered and controlling) — *ok w/ ths*
- Not quick-tempered (void of anger that becomes sinful) — *''*
- Not pugnacious (not abusive) — *''*
- Gentle (sensitive, loving, and kind) — *''*
- Peaceable (nonargumentative and nondivisive) — *a little more*
- Free from the love of money (nonmaterialistic) — *ok*
- Manages his own household well (a good husband and father) — *rt/a. imprt.*
- Loving what is good (pursues godly activities) — *ok*
- Just (wise, discerning, nonprejudiced, and fair) — *ok*
- Devout (holy, devoted to God) — *ok*
- Self-controlled (disciplined) — *2.*

Goals for Every Christian Man

When you look casually at this list of spiritual qualifications, you might conclude that Paul was *exclusively* outlining qualifications for men who serve in pastoral and teaching positions in the church. Not so! Rather, Paul was in essence saying to both Timothy and Titus that if a man wants to become a spiritual leader, that's great. Just make sure he's well on his way in becoming a man who is more and more measuring up to "the stature which belongs to the fullness of Christ." Paul then outlined how we can determine if he is this kind of man, using these specific qualities of maturity.

In other words, these qualities should be *goals for every Christian man* who is a Christ-follower. Inspired by the Holy Spirit, Paul pulled together a number of characteristics he and other authors mentioned elsewhere in the New Testament for both men and women and outlined a marvelous profile for measuring Christ-like maturity in men particularly.

An Exciting Challenge

As you evaluate your life based on these qualities, be on guard against discouragement. See this as a great opportunity to become the man God really wants you to become. Remember that Satan may be looking over your shoulder and whispering in your ear, "You'll never become that kind of man. You've blown it too badly. There's no hope for you. You'll never break out of your old sin patterns."

When Satan tempts you with these thoughts, meditate on the words which were penned by the half brother of Jesus Christ:

> Submit therefore to God. Resist the devil and he will flee from you. Draw near to God and He will draw near to you. (James 4:7–8a)

Listen to God's voice saying, "I love you no matter what you've done, no matter where you are in your spiritual growth, no matter what your feelings. I'm on your side. I have not rejected you. You are My child. You *can* become a man of God, and I'm here to help you."

Thinking and Growing Together

The final section in this chapter and the ones to follow is designed for discussion involving two or more individuals who meet to clarify the concepts in each chapter and to apply biblical truths in their daily lives. Here are some important guidelines:

Suggestions for Discussion and Application

renewal.tv/mm1r

First, make sure someone is appointed to be the servant-leader. This is particularly important if there are more than two in a group. Members of the group may want to take turns serving in this role, which can be arranged ahead of time or done spontaneously.

Second, schedule time to share each individual's "greatest learning" from each chapter.

Third, use the questions in this chapter and in the chapters to follow for more in-depth discussion:

life's career
& character

- Why do some men grow rapidly in their Christian faith once they become believers, and why do others struggle, seemingly taking as many steps backward as forward?

  Note: Think of examples you can sensitively share. You may want to share your own personal experiences.

- As you look back at Paul's Maturity Profile on page 21–22, what would you consider to be your areas of strength?

  Note: Take time to do this personally and then allow each man to share his thoughts with others.

- As you look at the same profile, in what one specific area would you like to grow the most? What factor or factors may be holding you back?

  Note: Take time to do this personally and then again share your thoughts with others.

Set Goals

Write out one goal you'd like to achieve as a result of this study.

Hospitality

Singleness - connected w fone wife (purity)

Pray for One Another

Once each man has written out a goal, allow time to share the goals with others and to pray for each other.

Note: No one in the group should feel forced to share or pray. On the other hand, no one should be excluded from participating.

2

Building a Good Reputation

Above reproach

1 Timothy 3:2; Titus 1:6

A Conversation I'll Never Forget

When my oldest daughter, Renee, was about eight years old, I was preparing a message on "the family." I asked her if she would mind listening to what I was planning to share with the congregation the following Sunday. I also asked her if she would give me feedback on how my life as her father measured up to what I was going to share with the people in the church.

A Personal Message from Gene

renewal.tv/mm2i

I still remember my beautiful little daughter climbing up beside me on the couch in our living room. I began to share my message point by point. It was indeed an intimate moment. She listened intently, and then I noticed about halfway through she began fighting tears.

Needless to say, she had my attention! Concerned, I asked her if something in my life troubled her. I'll never forget her answer.

"Just one thing, Daddy," she responded softly and sensitively, as if she were fearful she'd hurt my feelings.

"What's that, honey?" I asked.

"Well," she responded, "sometimes when I talk to you, you don't listen."

Yes, Renee had my attention. My little daughter was talking about one of my weaknesses. My tendency was not to listen when my children were trying to communicate. This was particularly true when they were young. In that special and vulnerable moment, Renee told me that at times she tried to share with me some things that were really important to her. She was also saying she knew by the look in my eyes that my mind was a thousand miles away—resolving a problem at the office, thinking through a message outline, or concentrating on my own agenda. I did not realize she had been waiting all day long to tell me something exciting that was happening in her own life.

I wish I could say that Renee's comments that day totally changed me. Through the years, I have had to fight the temptation as both a husband and a father to at times be in my own world. Yes, it's easy to take those who are closest to us for granted. "They'll understand," we conclude. But the fact is they will conclude we simply don't have time for them—that we're not interested.

One thing is for certain! That experience with my little daughter made me aware of my weakness and helped me set some new goals that hopefully have changed me from that day forward. I have never forgotten that experience, and I have worked hard to be a better father. And today, my grandchildren have given me opportunities to continually grow in this area of my life—to have a "good reputation" with those closest to me—as well as other people in my life.

An Overarching Quality

When Paul stated that a mature man is "above reproach" in his letters to Timothy and Titus, fortunately he was not referring to perfection (1 Tim. 3:2; Titus 1:6). Rather, he was simply stating that we should have a *good reputation*. Furthermore, it's an overarching characteristic. It's a summary quality—the result of living out the other qualities mentioned in these two lists (1 Tim. 3:1–7; Titus 1:5–10).

Exp. worky thru comit his clantin LA.

Find Us Seven Good Men

Being "above reproach" or having a good reputation is not a new idea in the New Testament. When the church faced its first organizational problem in Jerusalem, the apostles recommended that "*seven men of good reputation*" be selected to help solve the problem of food distribution among the Grecian widows (see Acts 6:3).

This was a delicate situation. The church was expanding rapidly, and consisted of both believing Jews who lived in the area of Jerusalem and Judea as well as God-fearing Grecian Jews who had come from all over the Roman world for a fifty-day celebration. On the last day—the Day of Pentecost—the Holy Spirit came to the apostles particularly. As a result, many Jews in both groups put their faith in the Lord Jesus as their Messiah. Furthermore, many who had come from other places decided to stay in Jerusalem to see what was going to happen next.

This created a crisis. The God-fearing Grecian Jews who came from afar ran out of food first—and even though believers from both groups were very generous, the tendency was to neglect the Grecian widows who had become believers.

The apostles knew they needed to appoint men of integrity to care for this need. They would only make the problem worse if they delegated this task to men who were not respected in the Christian community. They needed to be men who had a "good reputation"—men who wouldn't show favoritism. This is why the

28

apostles asked the Grecian Jews themselves to select these men from their own ethnic background. They alone would be aware of those who had this kind of integrity.

"Well Spoken Of"

Paul and Barnabas had come to Timothy's hometown on the first missionary journey. They had already planted churches in Pisidia Antioch and Iconium, but had to leave because of persecution. But in Lystra, the persecution became so intense that Paul was stoned, dragged outside the city, and left for dead.

According to Luke's account in the book of Acts, a group of disciples—those who became believers—gathered around Paul. It's only logical to conclude that young Timothy stood in that circle along with his grandmother, Lois, and his mother Eunice. And as the group stood there mourning, God raised Paul up and he and Barnabas continued their missionary journey (see Acts 13:14–14:20).

It takes time to build a good reputation.

As Paul's missionary story unfolded, he returned to Lystra on his second journey—where he evidently first heard about young Timothy's conversion and spiritual growth. Luke has recorded that *"he was well spoken of by the brethren who were in Lystra and Iconium"* (Acts 16:2). In other words, Timothy was "above reproach," even as a relatively new Christian. Even though his father was an unbeliever, he had continued to grow in his Christian faith (2 Tim. 3:14–16).

Note three things about Timothy's reputation:

1. People were talking about this young man ("he was well spoken of").
2. Several were talking about Timothy's reputation ("the brethren").
3. They were talking about Timothy in more than one location ("in Lystra and Iconium").

What we know from Timothy's story teaches us a very important principle. When understanding and applying what Paul meant by the quality of being "above reproach," we must remember that people who have good reputations create positive conversations among a variety of people in various locations.

What Are Others Saying About You?

It takes time to build a good reputation. But whatever our background, we should make it a goal. It will happen naturally if we're growing and maturing in our Christian lives. Conversely, a Christian who has a poor reputation is demonstrating traits that are not in harmony with Christian principles, nor is his lifestyle in harmony with what people naturally expect from a man who claims to be a Christ-follower.

This entire study is designed to help us develop a godly reputation. A good place to start is to determine what people actually think of us—right now.

Points of Action

- Do I get positive feedback from those closest to me (my wife, my children, my friends) that would indicate I have a good reputation?

Remember, feedback from those who do not know you well is not necessarily a good test. Their judgments can be superficial. They may be impressed with your physical appearance, your speaking ability, your "platform," or public personality, which may or may not represent who you really are as a person.

For example, how well do you know me? Merely reading this book or watching my video messages will not give you a true understanding of my reputation. You might be impressed with what I say, how I say it, or what appears to be a commitment to godly living. But how do you know what I am really like? The truth is, you probably don't—unless you've talked with people who have observed my life over a period of time in a variety of situations.

Over the years I've had many opportunities to speak to people all over the world—people I've never met before or have only met casually. In these situations, I could easily fake spirituality. Unfortunately, this has been done by some well-known Christian personalities. It's easy to be impressed with a person's public personality, but that may or may not be what that individual is like in private.

I say this not to make you skeptical or judgmental. But if you really want to know what I am like, you'll have to talk to those who really know me. You will need to ask my wife, who has lived with me for many years. You will need to talk to my children, who grew up in our home and now have homes of their own. You will want to talk to the elders in the churches I've started and pastored—men who have ministered with me for a number of years.

How Well Do You Know Me?

Please understand! I'm still in process. In fact, as I pen these words I'm convicted by some of my own inconsistencies. But I'm thankful for a group of men in my life who have helped me set goals for my life—attitudes and actions that reflect Jesus Christ. They've helped me practice what I preach and when I violate God's will, I've learned to acknowledge my failures and then once again proceed to walk in the will of God. I *do* want to finish well! To test the reality of this confession, I invite you to talk to those who have known me well for many years.

A Special Note of Thanks

At this point I'd like to say a special word of appreciation to the men who have endorsed this edition of *The Measure of a Man*.

I've known these brothers for many years—and most of them have served closely with me. I do indeed appreciate their trust.

Thanks, brothers, for affirming my own personal walk with Christ.

Over the years I've been invited to teach at various theological schools. As an assignment, I've asked my students to read through *The Measure of a Man* with either their spouse or a close friend and to ask this person to help them evaluate their lives in the light of the biblical qualities of maturity.

Once they have completed the assignment, I've asked them to outline their strengths as well as the areas where they believe they need to grow and improve. Invariably, these students have reported that this has been the most significant and life-changing assignment they have ever completed. The reason, I believe, is obvious. They have come face-to-face with what God says about biblical maturity, and they've taken an honest look at where they are in measuring up to "the stature which belongs to the fullness of Christ." They've taken another step in discovering "what the will of God is, that which is good and acceptable and perfect" (Rom. 12:2).

How Well Do You Know Yourself?

To personalize this study, you will need to do the same research about yourself. If you really want to know what kind of reputation you have—what people really think of you—ask your own wife (if married), and then give her freedom to answer the question openly and objectively. Ask your children and then give them the freedom to do the same. Ask those who know you well in your church and those who know you in the business world. You'll be amazed at what you'll learn. Is it threatening? Yes. But it will be well worth it in terms of results.

Some Additional Questions

- Do people seek me out to share their lives with me? Do people trust me with confidential information?

- Do my relationships with people grow deeper and more significant the longer they know me and the closer they get to me? Or do my friendships grow strained and shallow as people learn what I am really like?
- Does my circle of friends grow continually wider and larger? Do an increasing number of people admire and trust me?
- Do people recommend me for significant or difficult tasks without fear of my letting them down? *yes, emphatically.*

Taking the Plunge

If you find it difficult to be objective about the answers to the previous questions or to get started, sit down with your spouse or a close male friend and ask her or him to help you honestly evaluate the answers.

I realize this is a threatening assignment. It's not easy to do. In fact, it's like standing on a cliff getting ready to dive into waters you've never explored before—even though you know of others who have gone before you. As one who has been there, I'd like to encourage you to take the plunge. I assure you that it will change your life and how people feel about you. Being willing to go through this process will in itself begin to positively build your reputation.

Thinking and Growing Together

This section is designed for group discussion and personal application after reading and studying the content of this chapter.

Suggestions for Discussion and Application

renewal.tv/mm2r

First, make sure someone is appointed to take the lead.

Second, spend time sharing your "greatest learning" from this chapter.

Third, use the following questions for more in-depth discussion.

- What is the first step we can take as men to determine what people really think of us? *Get rid of social media*
- Are there areas in our lives where we believe people have false views of us and have misjudged our attitudes and actions? Why has this happened? What can we do to correct this misperception without appearing to be defensive?
- Are we aware of any attitudes and actions in our lives right now that are hurting our reputations? What steps can we take immediately to rebuild our reputations in those particular areas?
- What one thing would you like to do immediately to begin to enhance your reputation as a Christian man?

Set a Goal

Write out one goal you'd like to achieve as a result of this study.

_____

_____

_____

_____

_____

_____

_____

Pray for One Another

Once each man has written out a goal, allow time to share the goals with others and to pray for each other.

Note: No one in the group should feel forced to share or pray. On the other hand, no one should be excluded from participating.

3

Maintaining Moral Purity

The husband of one wife
1 Timothy 3:2; Titus 1:6

Abusing God's Gift

I remember meeting a young family man several years ago (let's call him "Jose") when I was ministering in a South American country. When he was just a young boy, entering the age of puberty, his father took him to a prostitute and offered her money to teach his son everything there was to know about sex. In addition, the father put this woman on a retainer, so his son could visit her anytime he wished. Hard to imagine? Yes, but it's true and common in that particular culture.

A Personal Message from Gene

renewal.tv/mm3i

You can predict what happened. Jose became addicted to this kind of lifestyle. Eventually, when he grew older, he decided to get married and have children. Like so many of his friends who grew up in that society, he continued to visit a prostitute regularly, even after he was married. And like so many women in that culture, his wife knew about his extramarital activities. She accepted it, though reluctantly, as normal behavior among men.

Then something very dramatic happened. Jose became a true Christ-follower. As a believer, he discovered for the first time the biblical standard for morality and marriage. To continue his association with the prostitute, or any woman other than his wife, would be to continue to sin against God as well as his wife and family. Unfortunately and predictably, his addiction was so powerful that he continually struggled to measure up to this biblical standard.

When I met Jose, he had been victorious over his sin for several months. Through Bible study, prayer, and understanding his true identity in Jesus Christ and the power of the Holy Spirit—as well as being accountable for his actions—he was finally able to conquer the temptation when he left his office after work. Rather than making his regular visits to a prostitute, he returned home and spent the evenings with his wife and family.

Two Thousand Years Ago

If you can understand the dynamics in this story, you can also understand more clearly what happened regularly in the New Testament culture, especially among Gentiles.

Three-Women Men

It was common in the Roman world for affluent men to have at least three women in their lives. One woman was a slave girl who lived in the same house or compound who was always available to her master for sexual pleasure. Another woman was a prostitute down at the pagan temple, which was considered a religious rite in the various pagan religions. The other woman was the man's wife,

37

the one who would help carry on the family name by giving birth to children and taking the primary responsibility for rearing them. *Who could tolerate such behavior?* you ask. Good question. But the fact is that these women had little choice about these circumstances. Their very lives and sustenance depended on their full cooperation.

Morality Today

Many of us who live in countries that have been deeply influenced by Hebrew-Christian morality find it difficult to comprehend these social dynamics. However, people who grow up in cultures guided by a different value system from ours come to accept this kind of lifestyle, like it or not.

I remember talking to a young woman from an Eastern country. She related a story similar to the one I have just told. "How can this be?" I asked. She responded, "The women in our society are very tolerant of their husbands' extramarital behavior."

This is the kind of culture in which the apostle Paul preached the gospel. And it was in this kind of culture that men came to Christ. For the first time in their lives, they heard God's message regarding moral purity. God's plan for each of them was to have only one woman in their lives—a wife.

God's Truth Penetrates Culture

Many of these New Testament men had the same problems and temptations in their lives as men who come to Christ in similar cultures today. Although they hear and understand Christ's message of living morally, changes often come slowly. The power of sexual addiction often controls them, even after they have become believers.

In the Roman world, Paul was concerned that a man who did not have victory over sexual immorality should never be appointed to lead others in the church. Therefore, Paul told Timothy that a spiritual leader must be "the husband of one wife"—or more literally, "a man of one woman."

If you have difficulty understanding this reality, consider the Corinthians. They tolerated and even bragged about a man who had a sexual relationship with his stepmother, an act of immorality that wasn't even practiced in the pagan community (1 Cor. 5:1). Furthermore, listen to Paul's more complete description of the Corinthians' lifestyle before they became believers:

> On the contrary, you yourselves wrong and defraud. You do this even to your brethren. Or do you not know that the unrighteous will not inherit the kingdom of God? Do not be deceived; neither fornicators, nor idolaters, nor adulterers, nor effeminate, nor homosexuals, nor thieves, nor the covetous, nor drunkards, nor revilers, nor swindlers, will inherit the kingdom of God. Such were some of you; but you were washed, but you were sanctified, but you were justified in the name of the Lord Jesus Christ and in the Spirit of our God. (1 Cor. 6:8–11)

If Christians in the New Testament church continued to tolerate moral degeneracy, it's not surprising that Paul made sure all believers knew that a man of God, especially a Christian leader, should have only one woman in his life—his wife—and should be faithful to her and her alone. But Paul also spelled out the good news—that in Christ we're saved by grace through faith and we can be set free from these sinful behaviors. This is why he wrote to the believers in Rome: "What shall we say then? Are we to continue in sin so that grace may increase? May it never be! How shall we who died to sin still live in it?" (Rom. 6:1-2).

A Higher Standard Still

We must also remember that Christian morality extends its boundaries beyond the physical act of illegitimate sexual relationships. Here are the words of Jesus Christ:

You have heard that it was said, "You shall not commit adultery"; but I say to you that everyone who looks at a woman with lust for her has already committed adultery with her in his heart. (Matt. 5:27–28)

Lust Versus Temptation

"With lust for her" means not only to desire a woman in an illicit sexual relationship but also to think in terms of how to cause it to happen. This differentiates temptation from lust or sin.

For example, take David. When did he commit adultery? Was it when he first walked out on his balcony and noticed Bathsheba bathing below? Obviously he was tempted! At that moment, he had a choice. He could walk away. However, he chose to learn more about her. Who was this beautiful woman? And once he found out who she was, he sent for her and engaged in an illegitimate sexual relationship.

Only God knows our hearts, but it's clear that David committed adultery prior to the physical act. It no doubt happened at some point when temptation turned to lust; namely, when he decided to send for her. This illustrates what Jesus meant when He said—"I say to you, that everyone who looks at a woman with *lust for her* has committed adultery with her already in his heart" (Matt. 5:28).

Our Sexually Oriented Culture

Most every man, married or single, is sexually tempted. No one can avoid completely the sensuous messages that permeate our culture. It's not difficult to understand why men are tempted sexually on a regular basis. Perhaps the most devastating development has appeared on the internet. Explicit pornography is just a click away—and private.

But to be tempted is not a sin. Temptation, however, can quickly lead to sin. Any man who deliberately pursues an illegitimate sexual relationship with a woman in his mind has, in God's sight, already committed an immoral act.

In the world today, "fantasy" about women other than our wives is promoted as normal and natural and even necessary to have a fulfilling sex life. But Jesus's teaching is clear that this kind of fantasy world is off-limits for a man who desires to follow God fully.

Thankfully, the blood of Jesus Christ continues to cleanse us from all sin—if we are true believers (1 John 1:9). But if we are going to live and fellowship with the Lord—which means walking in His will—we must renew our minds on a regular basis and be transformed into Christ's image (Rom. 12:1–2).

Points of Action

When the group of men I initially met with interacted with this particular quality for measuring spiritual maturity, we discussed some practical steps we could take to be men of high moral integrity.

Step 1: Develop Good Communication

A married man who is able to keep his moral house in order and who is able to handle the normal temptations that arise in our contemporary culture is usually a man who has a fulfilling sex life.

ANOTHER CORINTHIAN PROBLEM

Paul spoke to this morality problem in 1 Corinthians 7:1–5. He instructed both wives and husbands to meet each other's sexual needs so that Satan would not lead one or the other into sexual immorality and unfaithfulness.

In view of Paul's instructions, it shouldn't surprise us that some married men become involved with other women, either mentally or physically, because of wives who are insensitive to their sexual and psychological needs. Some may be selfish or even hostile, using sex as a weapon. Or, more commonly, they may just be naive and unaware of the tremendous drives that can be triggered in men who face regular sexual temptations in the world in which they live.

But a word of caution! An unfulfilled sex life can become a rationalization. As men, we can quickly blame our wives for our out-of-control sexual desires. Furthermore, regardless of the circumstances, adultery is never justified in God's sight.

IF HE WERE MATURE, HE WOULDN'T BE TEMPTED

Communication is a two-way street that hopefully leads to mutual listening. The fact that a husband tries to share his needs doesn't guarantee a listening and understanding ear. I remember talking with a woman one day who, along with her husband, was involved in a Bible study with several other couples. The subject of sex surfaced. In the process, the men attempted to communicate their inner struggles with the way they normally think and respond.

> Communication is a two-way street that hopefully leads to mutual listening.

In my conversation with this woman, two things became apparent about her reactions to what the men had to say. *First*, she was highly threatened by the fact that her husband would even be sexually tempted. How could he be? In her mind, for him to even have spontaneous and momentary sexual thoughts about other women was sinful and mental adultery.

Clearly, this woman did not understand the difference between "temptation" and "lust." In our culture, men have little control over fleeting thoughts. Though we all have a sin nature, even as Christians, to be able to respond sexually to the opposite sex is a gift from God. However, we must not allow temptation to lead to the kind of lust Jesus described.

Second, I noticed that this woman had no concept whatsoever of how she differed from men in terms of temptation and response to sexual stimuli. She interpreted everything they were trying to communicate in terms of her own psychological and physiological perspectives and reactions.

Considering this woman's tendency to be threatened by her incorrect perceptions, it's easy to see why she had difficulty relating to what the men in this group were trying to communicate. A wife who responds this way when her husband attempts to communicate his struggles may close the door indefinitely for any kind of communication to occur. When this happens, the marriage is in serious trouble.

A PERSONAL STORY

I remember on one occasion I was traveling and stayed the night in an upscale hotel. I'd had a very busy and successful day in ministry, but when I found myself alone in my room, I noticed the movie advertisements on the top of the television set. It was clear that adult fare was readily available with the push of a button. Frankly, I was tempted. The very titles were designed to stimulate a man's sexual appetite.

As I was struggling with temptation, I picked up the phone and dialed my wife. I shared with her how I was feeling. "Why am I so tempted?" I asked. I'll never forget Elaine's response. "That's easy to understand," she responded with a sympathetic tone in her voice. "You're a man."

We then prayed together and asked God for strength not to yield to this kind of temptation. I remember falling asleep that night reading my Bible, realizing how fortunate I was to have a wife I could talk to—a woman who wasn't threatened and who encouraged me in those times of temptation.

Step 2: Avoid Sexually Stimulating Situations

Men should not set up conflict situations by deliberately exposing themselves to temptation. Several of the men in my initial study group also traveled extensively, and it was their consensus that airport newsstands featuring a variety of men's magazines are not conducive to moral purity. Neither are most hotel rooms where pornography is readily available. And to add to the problem, pornography is readily available on computers, smartphones, and tablets.

SOFT PORN PLAYS HARDBALL

Some Christian men rationalize what they watch on TV or the internet, or what they see in magazines, by avoiding X-rated viewing and limiting their activities to less explicit movies, or what is identified as "soft pornography." However, Dr. Judith Reisman has written a powerful book entitled *Soft Porn Plays Hardball* that demonstrates the effects this kind of sexual stimulus has on the millions of men who view this adult fare. In her book, Dr. Reisman demonstrates why allegedly innocent "girlie" magazines have done more harm to children, women, men,

> Nothing dulls a desire for communication with God and the study of His Word as much as indiscriminate exposure to illegitimate sexual stimuli.

and the family than has hardcore, illegal entertainment. She also documents how pornography bears an enormous responsibility for the spiraling rate of divorce, sexually transmitted diseases, and abortion, as well as new and deadly forms of sex crimes against women and children. The havoc wreaked on our culture is inestimable, and the family is the prime target.

Sadly, many Christian men have become addicted to this kind of pornography, which often leads them into more explicit kinds of viewing. And sadder still, the Christian family is not exempt from the damage this inflicts on wives and children.

PURSUE RIGHTEOUSNESS

A very important principle emerges from the study of Scripture: In the provocative society in which we live, and no matter what our spiritual maturity, we must guard against deliberately exposing ourselves to literature, movies, TV shows, websites, and activities of any kind that are designed to illegitimately excite and stimulate our sexual natures. This, of course, takes mental and spiritual discipline—which leads to the next step in maintaining moral purity.

Step 3: Think Right

Men should fortify themselves through regular study of the Word of God and prayer. Nothing dulls a desire for communication with God and the study of His Word as much as indiscriminate exposure to illegitimate sexual stimuli. And nothing is so effective in combating temptation and lust as a robust prayer life and Bible study program. Thus, the apostle Paul wrote,

> Finally, brethren, whatever is *true*, whatever is *honorable*, whatever is *right*, whatever is *pure*, whatever is *lovely*, whatever is of *good repute*, if there is any *excellence* and if anything worthy of *praise*, dwell on these things. (Phil. 4:8)

What Paul wrote to the Philippians is a great criteria by which all of us can evaluate what we read, see, and think. Does what we're doing pass this very specific biblical test?

Step 4: Be Accountable

Though these three previous steps are crucial in maintaining moral purity, every Christian man should also have at least one other Christian man as an accountability partner. This has become more and more necessary in the culture in which we live. This is particularly important when sexual temptations become intense and frequent. Even understanding wives should not be burdened with these persistent challenges. They can easily feel responsible for what is definitely a husband's problem.

We must remember, however, that having an accountability partner in itself is no guarantee that there will be true openness and honesty. For example, a pastor I knew well met with another pastor every week. However, he was not honest in his communication. In fact, he circumvented the tough questions we need to ask one another by simply saying, "We're mature men. Let's just talk." Unfortunately, he was having an affair and avoided real accountability. He eventually divorced his wife, married the other woman, and left the ministry.

Perhaps, as a single man, you are fighting a losing battle with lust. Of all people, you need an understanding friend and helper—a prayer partner, a listener, an adviser. But, never share your problems with a single girl or a married woman. That can be lethal. You need a mature man of God who can help you work through your problems.

Step 5: Seek Professional Counseling

Men should seek help from a competent Christian counselor if moral problems persist. This is particularly important and absolutely essential if a man has a sexual addiction. In these situations, a man needs someone other than his wife to help him overcome his problem. No matter how mature our marital partners, addictions are threatening to any woman.

A Special Assignment

Points of Action

The following projects are designed to help you maintain a life of moral purity:

- If married, ask your wife to read this chapter on her own. State that your purpose is to get her personal feedback and to form a common basis for discussion.
- Next, discuss the chapter with your wife, using the following questions as guidelines:

1. How do you as a woman differ from me as a man, especially in your sexual feelings, needs, and attitudes?
2. How do I as a man differ from you as a woman, especially in my sexual feelings, needs, and attitudes?
3. What can each of us do in our attitudes and behavior to better meet each other's needs sexually?

- If single, list three of the greatest problems you face that are related to your sexual nature. Then study these problems carefully and then honestly answer the following questions:
  1. What am I doing to accentuate these problems?
  2. What can I do on my own to solve these problems?
  3. Can I solve all of these problems alone, or do I need help from a competent counselor?
- Whether married or single, pray and ask the Lord to help you find another Christian man who will be your accountability partner.

Thinking and Growing Together

This section is designed for group discussion and personal application after reading and studying the content of this chapter.

Suggestions for Discussion and Application

renewal.tv/mm3r

First, make sure someone is appointed to take the lead.

Second, spend time sharing your "greatest learning" from this chapter.

Third, use the following questions for more in-depth discussion.

- Why does Paul in both his letters to Timothy and Titus list moral purity—"the husband of one wife"—immediately following "above reproach" (see 1 Tim. 3:2 and Titus 1:6)?

- What are some specific things that have worked in our lives to maintain moral purity? What hasn't worked?
- What are some things we can do to begin communicating with our wives? How can we be honest without our wives feeling threatened?

  Note: In communicating with your wife, you may need guidance and wisdom from a mature counselor—such as your pastor. This step needs to be taken very sensitively so as not to add to the problems and misunderstandings.

- Why do some men have more difficulty in maintaining moral purity?
- How can we avoid sexual addiction? If this is already a problem, how can we overcome it?

Set a Goal

Write out one goal you'd like to achieve as a result of this study.

Figure out how to get a wife ?
or companionship ? ? ?

Pray for One Another

Once each man has written out a goal, allow time to share the goals with others and to pray for each other.

Note: No one in the group should feel forced to share or pray. On the other hand, no one should be excluded from participating.

Our Lord has shown me how not to fall into this trap, so I do not resent the events of last year and where I am now. It improves a friendship with a woman without the danger of lust taking over.

In this way I have a chance at a help mate who is on the page of purity with me. At my age what is the use of this lust, but to be selfish?

4

Living a Balanced Life

Temperate

1 Timothy 3:2

This World Is Not Our Real Home!

I was speaking at a Bible conference, and during the coffee break, a woman began to talk nervously about the way our society is deteriorating—how things are going from bad to worse. I sensed an unusual amount of fear and insecurity. Clearly she was obsessed with the idea that our nation is falling apart morally and economically. Without much thought, I responded: "If you think it's bad now, just wait a while."

A Personal Message from Gene

renewal.tv/mm4i

Predictably, I didn't add to this person's sense of well-being. I could almost hear a gasp as she blurted out—"Oh, God wouldn't allow that to happen to America, would He?"

"Why not?" I asked. "Why wouldn't God allow bad things to happen in America? After all, we know from history that every nation that has departed from God's standard of righteousness has deteriorated and eventually collapsed."

Frankly, I wasn't trying to be insensitive, although if I had the opportunity to redo the conversation, I'd try to be more diplomatic in making my point—that our hope should *not* be based on how well things are going in our society. According to the Scriptures, we are just "strangers" passing through (1 Pet. 2:11). "Our citizenship is in heaven" (Phil. 3:20). This world is not our real home.

Spiritual and Emotional Stability

In actuality, this believer in Jesus Christ was expressing emotions that we've all held, especially in view of the dramatic cultural changes that are taking place in our society. However, this person's insecure response to these challenges in our society illustrates the opposite of what Paul meant when he penned the word *nephaleos*, which can be translated "temperate" or "sober" or "alert." He was describing Christ-followers who have a clear focus on life and who don't live in a constant state of anxiety because of world conditions. In other words, temperate biblical Christians don't lose their physical, psychological, and spiritual orientation. Regardless of the changes that violate biblical values, they maintain stability and steadfastness.

Applied to this study, a temperate man has as his goal "the measure of the stature which belongs to the fullness of Christ" (Eph. 4:13). He understands where history is going. He is aware that God is in control of the universe as well as the affairs of all humankind. However, he also knows he is responsible to do all he can to carry out God's purposes in the world. If married, his goal is to be a loving husband, a responsible father, and a good provider for his family. He is a devoted member of his church and a faithful employer or employee. His consistent objective is to be a dynamic Christian witness wherever he is by the way he lives and by what he says.

As a temperate man, he also doesn't go to extremes. On the one hand, he doesn't get bogged down trying to solve all of the world's problems. At the same time, he does what he can to solve social ills, but without neglecting biblical priorities.

As a temperate man, he doesn't go on emotional tangents. He relies on God for a sense of inner peace and security, no matter what is happening in the world. This doesn't mean he never has periods of anxiety, but overall he has a sense of stability. In the words of James, he is not a "double-minded man, unstable in all his ways" (1:8).

As a temperate man, he is a man of prayer. He takes Paul's exhortation to the Philippians seriously.

> Be anxious for nothing, but in everything by prayer and supplication with thanksgiving let your requests be made known to God. And the peace of God, which surpasses all comprehension, will guard your hearts and your minds in Christ Jesus. (Phil. 4:6–7)

A Proper Focus

Today, it's easy for all of us to get sidetracked onto peripheral issues. We can become so obsessed with the problems in our society that we spend most of our time and energy trying to clean up "the outside of the plate" and forget that it's what is on the inside that must be changed.

Don't misunderstand. I love my country, and I'm sure you do, too. I hope it will be strong and secure for years to come. But God never intended for our earthly home to be our source of security. No matter what happens down here on Earth, we have hope in Jesus Christ. He is our true source for stability and security in life.

On the other hand, when I stop and think about what is *really* happening in our culture, I'm deeply concerned. I can get particularly anxious when I think about my children and grandchildren and what they will no doubt face in years to come. Yet when I stop to consider that God is still God and that He is in control of the universe and our nation, I once again refocus my thoughts and feelings and get back in balance. We are to be "light" and "salt" in a world that desperately needs Christ. The greatest contribution we can make is to be everything God wants us to be as individuals, as families, and as local churches. We'll then see people come to know Jesus Christ

> A temperate man relies on God for a sense of inner peace and security, no matter what is happening in his life.

and experience personal salvation. Perhaps God in His grace will bring renewal and revival to our nation.

Political Involvement

This does not mean that a temperate man is not a good citizen. As believers who live in a free society, we should do our best to be well informed. We should take the opportunities we have to voice our opinions through the political process—a marvelous opportunity we have in the western culture. We should speak out when we have a platform to do so.

But at the same time, we must be realistic without being pessimistic. The world loves darkness more than light. Generally, those who have chosen to rely on their own wisdom will not listen to God's wisdom. And if they do not listen, God will judge our nation.

But remember, if we have put our faith in the Lord Jesus Christ, our salvation is secure, no matter what happens around us. Furthermore, God has promised never to leave us or forsake us, regardless of our circumstances (see Heb. 13:5). This is why New Testament Christians could be joyful in the midst of trials and tribulations (see 1 Pet. 1:3–9).

Becoming Temperate

When Paul wrote to the Thessalonians, he gave us a wonderful contextual commentary regarding how to become "temperate." Though written in the first century, Paul's message is timeless. His metaphors are understandable and applicable today in all cultures of the world.

> Now as to the times and the epochs, brethren, you have no need of anything to be written to you. For you yourselves know full well that the day of the Lord will come just like a thief in the night. While they are saying, "Peace and safety!" then destruction will come upon them suddenly like labor pains upon a woman with child, and they will not escape. But you, brethren, are not in darkness, that the day would overtake you like a thief; for you are all sons of light and sons of day. We are not of night nor of darkness; so then let us not sleep as others do, but let us be *alert* and *sober* [temperate]. For those who sleep do their sleeping at night, and those who get drunk get drunk at night. But since we are of the day, let us be *sober* [temperate], having put on the breastplate of *faith* and *love*, and as a helmet, the *hope* of salvation. (1 Thess. 5:1–8)

In this New Testament letter Paul listed three keys to becoming temperate. Here they are:

First, to become temperate men we must become *men of faith*.

Saving Faith

To become "men of faith," we must first of all be "saved through faith." Paul made this very clear in his letter to the Ephesians:

> For by grace you have been saved through faith; and that not of yourselves, it is the gift of God; not as a result of works, that no one may boast. (Eph. 2:8–9)

Paul—and other writers of Scripture—made it clear that we cannot earn our salvation! It is indeed a gift from God, a great truth Martin Luther learned—even as a seminary professor. And once he understood this great truth, it changed his life and helped bring transformation and reformation throughout the church world!

What this means is that we cannot become men who measure up to the stature of Jesus Christ without entering into a personal relationship with Christ Himself. It is our faith in His death and resurrection that enables us to inherit eternal life. The question is—have you received this gift by faith? If you have, the Bible says you are "born again" (see Jesus's conversation with Nicodemus in John chapter 3).

A Work of Faith

After Paul explained saving faith in Ephesians 2:8–9, he then described a work of faith in the next verse:

> For we are His workmanship, created in Christ Jesus for *good works*, which God prepared beforehand so that we would walk in them. (Eph. 2:10)

Once we have experienced saving faith that brings eternal life, we're ready to become men of faith who walk by faith. Like men of old, such as Abel, Noah, Abraham, Isaac, Moses, and others who are cataloged so dramatically in Hebrews 11, mature men of God step out and act on the promises of God. We become men of faith!

Let Us Run the Race

Notice the faith and action of each of these men:

- "By faith Abel *offered* . . . a better sacrifice than Cain" (11:4).
- "By faith Noah . . . *prepared* an ark" (v. 7).
- "By faith Abraham . . . *obeyed* by going out" (v. 8).
- "By faith Abraham . . . *offered* up Isaac" (v. 17).

- "By faith Isaac *blessed* Jacob" (v. 20).
- "By faith [Moses] *left* Egypt" (v. 27).

All of the Old Testament men listed here "died in faith, without receiving the promises, but having seen them and having welcomed them from a distance, and having confessed that they were *strangers* and *exiles* on the earth" (v. 13).

Let Us Fix Our Eyes on Jesus

Today our goal should be to become temperate men who believe God and act on His promises although we don't fully understand what lies ahead on this earth. We don't allow ourselves to be lulled to sleep but keep on looking for the second coming of Jesus Christ to deliver us from the wrath to come (see 1 Thess. 5:9). Furthermore, we encourage one another with this truth and help build up all members of the body of Christ by helping them to look forward to that day. By word and example, temperate Christ-followers practice the exhortation in Hebrews:

> Let us also lay aside every encumbrance and the sin which so easily entangles us, and let us run with endurance the race that is set before us, *fixing our eyes on Jesus, the author and perfecter of faith*. (12:1b–2b)

Second, to become temperate men we must become **men of hope.**

Hope refers to our *eternal inheritance*, which is laid up for us in heaven (see Col. 1:5; 1 Pet. 1:3–4). It's our *"hope* of salvation" (1 Thess. 5:8), "the *hope* of eternal life, which God, who cannot lie, promised long ages ago" (Titus 1:2). All of this will be fulfilled in a special way when we experience "the blessed *hope* and the appearing of the glory of our great God and Savior, Christ Jesus" (Titus 2:13).

Hope also refers to our steadfastness and stability. This is why Paul in his first letter to the Thessalonians thanked God for their "steadfastness of hope in our Lord Jesus Christ" (1 Thess. 1:3). They had fixed their hope "on the living God" (1 Tim. 4:10), rather than "on the uncertainty of riches" and the things of this world (6:17). They were holding fast to the confession of their "hope without wavering" (Heb. 10:23) and had fixed their "hope completely on the grace to be brought . . . at the revelation of Jesus Christ" (1 Pet. 1:13).

Men of hope are steadfast

Yes, the world around us is deteriorating. Sin is taking its toll. In terms of our cultural values, many of the liberal and so-called progressive people in our society want to remove all acknowledgements of God and His divine laws from all public display in our society. Many want to ban the Ten Commandments that are so visibly displayed in the Supreme Court and other prominent places. They want "In God We Trust" to be banished from our currency and the phrase "so help me God" never uttered in public ceremonies. They would be elated if the Bible was never used at a swearing-in ceremony for the president of our country.

This trend in our society has impacted us all. Divorces are multiplying. Families are becoming more and more dysfunctional and self-destructing. Sex outside of marriage is becoming the norm. Abortions continue to take the lives of thousands of unborn children every year. Homosexuality is rapidly becoming an acceptable lifestyle. Hard core pornography is readily available on our smartphones, tablets, and computers. Political corruption including dishonesty and even immorality permeate leadership activities at the highest level of the land. The drug culture is destroying lives with even marijuana becoming legalized. Materialism reigns and motivates millionaires and paupers to lie, steal, and engage in the worst kind of criminal activity.

These are indeed realities and it's not a pretty picture. We cannot look the other way. Those of us who understand history know how these behaviors have destroyed whole empires.

But the good news is that even though we're living in a decaying world, no matter what happens, **we have hope!** If we know the Lord Jesus Christ as our personal Savior, we have a secure place prepared for us in heaven that will never fade away (John 14:1–6). Furthermore, we can be men of hope in the midst of our decaying culture.

This takes us back once again to what Paul wrote to the Thessalonians. As we've seen, he used the concept of drunkenness to illustrate the lack of temperance (1 Thess. 5:7). Though alcohol can certainly keep us from being mentally and physically stable and steadfast, Paul was making a point that applies to all we do and anything that keeps us from being temperate. For example, we can become drunk from the things of this world. We can stumble in the darkness of sin rather than walk in the light of God's truth. But with God's divine help we can "be alert and sober [temperate]" (1 Thess. 5:6).

Third, to become temperate men, we must become **men of love.**

Paul also understood the importance of this quality in his letter to the Corinthians. Culminating in Chapter 13, he wrote:

But now *faith, hope, love,* abide these three; but *the greatest of these is love.* (1 Cor. 13:13)

Earlier in this chapter, Paul defined love very specifically:

• Love is patient,
• Love is kind and
• Love is not jealous;
• Love does not brag and

- Love is not arrogant,
- Love does not act unbecomingly;
- Love does not seek its own,
- Love is not provoked,
- Love does not take into account a wrong suffered,
- Love does not rejoice in unrighteousness, but
- Love rejoices with the truth (13:4–6).

Love, then, is really the capstone for *faith*, because love "believes all things" (v. 7)—that is "all things" that are true and revealed by God. Love is also the capstone for *hope*, because love "hopes all things" (v. 7)—that is "all things" that are promises from God. Furthermore, love is the greatest, because it "never fails" (v. 8)— that is love that is based on God's character and what He has done for us (see John 3:16).

Points of Action

The following project is designed to help you develop the quality of temperance.

Some Probing Questions

Answer the following questions as honestly as you can.

- *How strong is my faith in God and His Word?* Do I *really* believe He exists and that Jesus Christ is coming again? If I do, how is my faith revealed in my *actions*?
- *How aware am I of the hope of my calling* (see Eph. 1:18)? How fully do I understand "the riches of the glory of His inheritance in the saints, and what is the surpassing greatness of His power toward us who believe" (vv. 18–19)? Have

I fixed my hope on the things of this world or on eternal values (see Matt. 6:33)?

- *Am I a man of love?* How well do I measure up to the criteria described in 1 Corinthians 13? Am I patient? Am I kind? Am I generous? Am I humble? Am I courteous? Am I unselfish? Am I controlled? Am I pure in motives? Am I sincere?

Yes on all counts except sincerity. Am I Manipulative

Thinking and Growing Together

This section is designed for group discussion and personal application after reading and studying the contents of this chapter:

Suggestions for Discussion and Application

First, make sure someone is appointed to lead the group.

Second, spend time sharing your "greatest learning" from this chapter.

renewal.tv/mm4r

Third, use the following questions for more in-depth discussion.

- What are some specific ways we can become men of *faith*, *hope*, and *love* in our present cultural situation?
- How can we keep balance in our lives when we face so many pressures in our changing society? How can we determine if we are getting too caught up in the issues in our society? How can we determine if we are not active enough in addressing these issues?
- How can we help our pastor maintain balance in these areas?
- What are some specific ways we can determine if we are growing in faith, hope, and love?

Set a Goal

Write out one goal you'd like to achieve as a result of this study.

Less manipulative + honest about fears

attaining courage in a crucial time in the fallen world -- + not make time a cruciality dictate my emotions + behavior.

Pray for One Another

Once each man has written out a goal, allow time to share the goals with others and to pray for each other.

Note: No one in the group should feel forced to share or pray. On the other hand, no one should be excluded from participating.

5

Demonstrating Wisdom

Prudent

1 Timothy 3:2

"The Wise in Heart Shall Be Called Prudent"
(Prov. 16:21 KJV)

I had the privilege of knowing the late Dr. William Culberson, who served for a number of years as president of Moody Bible Institute in Chicago, Illinois. During the thirteen years I served on the Moody faculty, I not only had many personal conversations with this man, but I also observed his actions and reactions in a variety of situations. I sat with him in hundreds of faculty meetings,

A Personal Message from Gene

renewal.tv/mm5i

listening to his sage advice and wise comments. I heard him open the Word of God in chapel sessions, making the Scriptures practical and applicable to our lives, as faculty members and as students. I played hours of power volleyball on our faculty team, sometimes with him and sometimes against him. Intense athletic competition reveals a man's true character like no other activity.

As I reflect on my associations with Dr. Culberson, I remember a very wise man. The late Dr. Wilbur Smith, who served with Dr. Culberson on a special Bible translation team, once commented that this man's greatest strength was to be able to listen to everyone express opinions and then give the correct answer with clarity and great wisdom. Dr. Smith's comment reminds me of the following Proverb:

> A wise man will *hear* and increase in learning. (Prov. 1:5)

Sound Judgment

The word Paul used in the Greek text to describe this quality of maturity is *sophron*, which is translated into English with a variety of words, such as being sober minded, sensible, and prudent. Clearly it means to have a "sound mind" or to have "sound judgment."

One of my favorite passages of Scripture explaining what Paul had in mind when he used this word is in his letter to the Romans:

> For through the grace given to me I say to every one among you not to think more highly of himself than he ought to think; but to think so as to have *sound judgment* [to think *soberly*, *sensibly*, or *prudently*], as God has allotted to each a measure of faith. (12:3)

Paul was concerned that we have a proper view of ourselves in relationship to God and to other Christians (see Rom. 12:4–8). Evidently, some believers in Rome—as well as in Corinth (see 1 Cor. 12:14–27)—had an overly exalted view of their positions in the body of Christ. Consequently, Paul exhorted them to "be devoted to one another in brotherly love" and to "give preference to one another in honor" (Rom. 12:10).

More than any other characteristic of maturity, Paul related this concept to all members of the body of Christ. Within a span of five verses of Scripture, he instructed Titus to exhort older men, older women, younger women, and younger men to be "sensible" or "prudent" (see Titus 2:2–6).

Recognizing Prudence

Humility

A prudent man is a *humble* man who knows that all that he has (his gifts, abilities, and possessions) is from God. Without our Creator, we could not speak, write, walk, make decisions, or breathe. We would not be alive, and most of all, we would not have eternal life. As Paul wrote, God the Father sent His Son to be the Savior of the world. Knowing this, our goal should be to have the same attitude as Christ Jesus—to:

> Do nothing from selfishness or empty conceit, but with *humility of mind* regard one another as more important than yourselves; do not *merely* look out for your own personal interests, but also for the interests of others. (Phil. 2:3–4)

Gratitude

A prudent man also has a proper view of the *grace* of God. He knows that through God's "grace" he has "been saved through faith"—not by anything he has done. Consequently, he is motivated to live for Christ by this gracious gift of eternal life.

Paul's words to Titus should become a reality in all of our lives:

> For the *grace of God has appeared*, bringing salvation to all men, instructing us to deny ungodliness and worldly desires and to live *sensibly [prudently]*, righteously and godly in the present age. (Titus 2:11–12)

Prayerful

A prudent man is a man of prayer. He practices the apostle Peter's exhortation: "Be of *sound judgment [prudent]* and sober *spirit* for the *purpose of prayer*" (1 Pet. 4:7).

A prudent man knows that he needs God's power in his life in order to live a godly life—that he cannot reflect Christ's fullness in his own strength. The apostle Paul beautifully illustrates and exemplifies this need for God's strength in his prayer for the Ephesians:

> For this reason I bow my knees before the Father, from whom every family in heaven and on earth derives its name, that He would grant you, according to the riches of His glory, to be strengthened with power through His Spirit in the inner man, so that Christ may dwell in your hearts through faith; and that you, being rooted and grounded in love, may be able to comprehend with all the saints what is the breadth and length and height and depth, and to know the love of Christ which surpasses knowledge, that you may be filled up to all the fullness of God. Now to Him who is able to do far more abundantly beyond all that we ask or think, according to the power that works within us, to Him be the glory in the church and in Christ Jesus to all generations forever and ever. Amen. (Eph. 3:14–21)

Meekness Is Not Weakness

Having a correct perspective regarding our place in God's family does not mean we should be withdrawn and inhibited. It doesn't mean we should lack self-confidence and be burdened with a sense of worthlessness.

Timothy apparently had a problem in this area of his life. He felt intimidated by those who opposed God's work. Paul charged Timothy never to "be ashamed" (2 Tim. 1:8) either of the Lord or of the Lord's servants. Thus, Paul wrote to Timothy:

For God has not given us a spirit of timidity, but of power and love and *discipline* [*sophronismos*—of a *sound mind*, KJV]. (v. 7)

What Paul wrote to Timothy applies to all of us. As Christians, we should never be ashamed or intimidated. If we are truly prudent, we'll recognize that we are unworthy to be called children of God and members of the family of God. However, we can rise up from our knees and walk forward courageously on our spiritual journey, giving all glory and honor to Jesus Christ. Paul said it best:

> I have been crucified with Christ; and it is no longer I who live, but Christ lives in me; and the *life* which I now live in the flesh I live by faith in the Son of God, who loved me and gave Himself up for me. (Gal. 2:20)

Paul's Example

The apostle Paul never hesitated to commend himself when he was falsely accused and belittled. At the same time, however, he made sure he had pure motives and that these motives were understood—that he was defending himself because of what God had done in his life.

This is clear in Paul's second letter to the Corinthians. Some people questioned his apostleship as well as his motives, and those of Timothy who ministered with Paul in Corinth. Thus, he wrote, "For if we are beside ourselves, it is for God; if we are of *sound mind* [prudent], it is for you" (5:13). We might paraphrase Paul's comments as follows:

> You may think we are bragging and are proud. If it appears that way to you, it is really because of what God has accomplished in our lives. We are only glorifying the work of God in our own experiences. In other words, we want you to see us as sober, prudent, and sensible men—men who are humbly acknowledging that we are what we are because of God's marvelous grace. (see vv. 11–12)

Modeling Prudence Today

Earlier, we noted that the apostle Paul instructed Titus to "urge the young men to be sensible [*sophroneo*—prudent]" (Titus 2:6). Paul then described in greater detail what he meant.

> In all things show yourself to be *an example* of good deeds, with purity in doctrine, dignified, sound in speech which is beyond reproach, so that the opponent will be put to shame, having nothing bad to say about us. (vv. 7–8)

The Only Way to Learn

Without modeling biblical faith, our words can be hollow and even meaningless. This is why Paul told Titus not only to teach young men to be prudent, but also to demonstrate this quality in his own life. All people need real-life examples of God's divine message.

An Unforgettable Conversation

I had a very meaningful experience one day while I was thinking about the concept in this chapter. I was having breakfast with my son, Kenton, who at the time was a sophomore at Baylor University. Our conversation seemed to reach a deeper level than ever before. We were talking about a series of letters I had written to him, starting when he was in junior high school. Over a period of time I wrote seven letters, with each letter based on Paul's words to Timothy:

> Don't let anyone look down on you because you are young, *but set an example* for the believers in speech, in conduct, in love, in faith and in purity. (1 Tim. 4:12 NIV)

At one point in our conversation about these letters, Kenton shared something that really got my attention. "Dad," he said, "I want you to know you're my model, and I want to be like you."

At that moment I had two reactions. First, I was overwhelmed with gratitude to God. It was a humbling experience.

Second, Kenton's comment impacted my own commitment to imitate Jesus Christ—to finish well by being a godly model—not only to Kenton, but now to his four sons, my own grandsons.

Another Memory

As I penned these words regarding my son's comments, my mind drifted back to an experience I had as a teenager. I had a close friend whose father invited me to join him and his son on a trip to Chicago. For a young farm boy from a small town in Indiana, this was exciting. One thing about this trip remains indelibly impressed on my mind. This father took his son (and me) to see a movie and a "live show" in a theater on State Street. The father lied about our ages to get us in.

Need I say more! What a tragic example for my friend and me. Here was a father who deliberately introduced his son and another impressionable young man (me) to a world of sinful behavior we heretofore knew nothing about. Thankfully, I became a Christian a short time later, which counteracted this kind of bad model. But I've often wondered about my friend, who eventually married and had children of his own. What kind of example has he been to his son?

We Can't Be Perfect

At this point, I need to clarify something highly important. Paul is not teaching us that we have to be perfect. My son said something else to me that morning. "Dad," he explained, "I know you make mistakes. And so do I. But you're still my model."

This comment ministered to me as much, if not more, than his initial statement. We do make mistakes. Those who associate closely with me, especially my children, know that more than anyone. Our tendency to sin will not leave us until we meet Christ face to face in eternity. But it encouraged me to know that Kenton saw beyond my mistakes and my sins to my heart in order to see who I really wanted to be.

Points of Action

The Peril of the Pendulum

As Christians, it's easy to go to extremes. We can see ourselves as *nothing* or we can get caught up in an *exalted* view of ourselves. Both are out of balance. On the one hand, we should recognize that all we are and have is because of God's grace. On the other hand, we should understand that God has given us special gifts and abilities, and He wants us to use those gifts and abilities to accomplish His will in our lives.

Recognize that there are various reasons for this imbalance to exist and persist. The following checklist will help you to begin to isolate the reasons for this imbalance.

1. An unfortunate series of circumstances beyond human control
   - ☐ You've lost a parent or both parents.
   - ☐ You've had bad experiences in school or in the neighborhood.
   - ☐ There are negative influences from your family and friends.
   - ☐ Hereditary factors or physical illness has created feelings of inferiority.
   - ☐ Can you name other factors?
2. Incorrect teaching
   - ☐ You've been taught for so long that you are worthless that you actually feel and believe you are worthless.
   - ☐ You've tried so hard to eliminate selfish thoughts and desires that you have downgraded your self-image and the image of God in you.

☐ You have an incorrect view of forgiveness and being right with God. For example, you try to become nothing so that God will accept you.

☐ *Remember:* You can do nothing to become right with God. You cannot even become nothing. You must come to God just as you are and accept His free gift of salvation.

3. Parents who were unwise

☐ They withheld praise and attention, creating in you an unnatural thirst and desire for recognition.

☐ They gave you too much of a prominent position, creating an emotional need always to be first in line and in the limelight.

Too Little or Too Much

As a pastor, I have discovered that Christian parents at times withhold praise and attention from their children for fear they will create a prideful attitude. In actuality, when we withhold positive feedback, we create the problem we try so hard to avoid. We'll rear a child who will be starved for attention. Ironically, in these circumstances, children may also have a pride problem later in life, because they did not learn how to emotionally handle success.

- If you believe you have isolated the source of your problem, interact with someone you trust—someone who is wise and prudent.
- If you're having difficulty isolating the problem, do the same thing. Seek wisdom. Ask a wise person to help you develop perspective and to pray with you about your struggle.
- Set up specific goals for your life to develop a proper self-image.

Be careful not to rationalize immature behavior on the basis of past circumstances and experiences. Become a responsible person.

Never blame your problems on someone else, including your parents, though they may have contributed to the problems.

Ask God to help you overcome your problems. Remember that the Word of God says:

> But if any of you lacks wisdom, let him ask of God, who gives to all generously and without reproach, and it will be given to him. (James 1:5)

Thinking and Growing Together

This section is designed for group discussion and personal application after reading and studying the contents of this chapter:

Suggestions for Discussion and Application

renewal.tv/mm5r

First, make sure someone is appointed to lead the group.

Second, spend time sharing your "greatest learning" from this chapter.

Third, use the following questions for more in-depth discussion.

- Which passage of Scripture referred to in this chapter meant the most to you? Why?
- What specific struggles face us in being men of wisdom?
- How can we be meek in our relationships without being weak?
- What personal experiences can we share with each other that will help us to encourage one another, pray for one another, love each other more, and build up one another?

Set a Goal

Write out one goal you'd like to achieve as a result of this study.

_____

_____

_____

_____

_____

_____

_____

Pray for One Another

Once each man has written out a goal, allow time to share the goals with others and to pray for each other.

Note: No one in the group should feel forced to share or pray. On the other hand, no one should be excluded from participating.

6

Making God's Truth Attractive

Respectable

1 Timothy 3:2

Cosmetics to the Gospel

When my family and I moved to Dallas, we built a home in the White Rock section of the city—which posed a problem. Yes, we "built our house on rock," but we had a terrible time putting in a lawn.

I remember one day in August when it was about 105 degrees. I was perspiring profusely while I was picking up rocks and trying to prepare the lot for topsoil. Barbie, an eight-year-old neighbor, had been watching me for several days. As she stood there sucking on her lollipop, she made a comment I'll never forget: "My mommy says you work awfully hard for a preacher!"

A Personal Message from Gene

renewal.tv/mm6i

I've laughed about this little girl's comment many times. But I'm also grateful. You see, I knew I had impressed her parents and perhaps changed their view of "preachers." This was an important step in becoming a witness for Christ. As some neighbors enjoyed saying, they didn't see me as a typical "man of the cloth."

The Greek Word *Kosmios*

The New Testament word *kosmios* is variously translated in 1 Timothy 3:2 as being "of good behavior," "well behaved," or "respectable." In essence, it's speaking of a man who is living a well-ordered life.

Our English word "cosmetics" comes from the same word. We see this connection when the verb *kosmeo* is translated "to adorn." For example, when Paul wrote to Titus, he urged slaves "to be subject to their own masters in everything" (2:9). They were "to be well-pleasing, not argumentative" (v. 9), and they were not to steal from their masters (see v. 10). Rather, they were to "*adorn* [*kosmeo*] the doctrine of God our Savior in every respect" (v. 10). In essence, their lives were to be like "cosmetics to the gospel."

Cosmetics, of course, are designed to make us attractive, to look and smell good. In other words, when non-Christians see respectability in our lives, hopefully they'll be attracted to the gospel message and to Jesus Christ.

A Modern Parable

A certain man and his wife in a particular city bought a home and moved in. This man was a Christian minister, and the man from whom he purchased the house was also a Christian minister.

In a few short days, it became apparent that some neighbors were disturbed that another minister had moved next door. For behold, the former minister had paid little attention to the outward appearance of his property. He allowed the grass to grow long, and when he did mow, certain sections were left uncut. And where he mowed, mounds of dry grass accumulated. Dandelions grew rampant, and other assorted weeds became a permanent part of the landscape. This man had planted no trees or shrubs, but allowed his large and spacious lawn to become a hay field.

It just so happened that certain neighbors in this particular community paid special attention to the outward appearances of their homes. True, many were not Christians, and they were materialistic. For some, their houses and their lawns appeared to be their gods.

Regardless of their own motives, these neighbors were totally disgusted by this minister's irresponsibility, lack of orderliness, and unwillingness to do his part to add to the natural beauty of the neighborhood. Consequently, the minister moving in after the former one found great communication barriers with his non-Christian neighbors. They were utterly convinced that Christians (ministers particularly) are a bad lot—irresponsible about keeping up their property and unconcerned about how this neglect affects their neighbors. The apostle Paul would identify this man as one who is *not respectable*.

The Interpretation

This parable is true. I was the man who bought this property from a minister and faced the communication barriers. Because of this man's reputation in the community, it took my wife and me many months to build trust with our neighbors. The way we accomplished it, however, was simple. Yet, it wasn't easy, because we had to prioritize our budget and do a lot of hard work.

What we needed to do first was apparent. We mowed regularly and sprayed the lawn to kill the weeds. Rather than fix up the inside of the house, we postponed that project and allocated money to buy shrubs and trees. And because of our limited budget, we dug the holes ourselves and planted everything. It was a huge task, but we got the job done. Would you believe that when the neighbors—particularly those who resented us the most—saw our efforts, they warmed up and became good friends?

I'm thankful for this experience because it taught me a great biblical and cultural lesson. If as Christians we choose to live in a particular neighborhood, we're also responsible to keep up our property so that we can be a good testimony to those who live there. This is part of being *respectable*—and a good witness for Jesus Christ.

Walking Worthy of Our Calling

A respectable man is a man whose lifestyle adorns the teachings of the Bible. Whether it's his dress, his speech, the appearance of his home, his office, or the way he does business—all are to be in harmony with biblical principles and doctrines. Because God is a God of order, a man of God should live an orderly life.

> A respectable man is a man who lives in such a way so that his total life adorns the teachings of the Bible.

When I think of being a man who lives a respectable life, I think of what Paul wrote to the Ephesian Christians both about our salvation experience and what should characterize our lives after we're saved. Here are his clear, succinct statements.

Regarding salvation:

For by grace you have been saved through faith; and that not of yourselves, it is the gift of God; not as a result of works, so that no one may boast. (Eph. 2:8–9)

Regarding our Christian lives:

For we are His workmanship, created in Christ Jesus for good works, which God prepared beforehand so that we would *walk* in them. (Eph. 2:10)

In spite of the clarity of Paul's teachings in these verses, these truths are perhaps the most misunderstood doctrines among professing Christians.

First of all, we cannot earn our salvation. It's a gift from God. Second, because of the gift of salvation and the Holy Spirit's power in our lives, we can engage in works that please God and reflect the fullness of Christ.

As we see in verse 10, Paul used a metaphor to describe our Christian life—a *walk* with Christ.

And later in chapter 4 of this letter, Paul went on to develop a Christian's "walk with Christ" in a very descriptive way:

> Therefore I, the prisoner of the Lord, implore you to *walk in a manner worthy of the calling* with which you have been called. (Eph. 4:1)

Clearly, our *calling* is our salvation experience as Paul described it generally in the first three chapters of this letter and specifically in Ephesians 2:8–9—that we're saved by God's grace through faith. Paul then went on to say that in view of this wonderful calling, we are to "walk in a manner worthy" of this wonderful gift of eternal life.

Paul followed these two general exhortations (in Eph. 2:10 and 4:1) with the following specific exhortations—using the same metaphorical word; that is, "to walk":

- So this I say, and affirm together with the Lord, that you *walk no longer just as the Gentiles also walk*, in the futility of their mind (Eph. 4:17).
- Therefore be imitators of God, as beloved children; and *walk in love*, just as Christ also loved you and gave Himself up for us, an offering and a sacrifice to God as a fragrant aroma (5:1–2).
- Therefore do not be partakers with them; for you were formerly darkness, but now you are Light in the Lord; *walk as children of Light* (vv. 7–8).
- Therefore *be careful how you walk*, not as unwise men but as wise, making the most of your time, because the days are evil (vv. 15–16).

Points of Action

The following project is designed to help you develop the quality of being respectable.

Ask Probing Questions

- What about my external appearance? Does it measure up to what is considered proper both biblically and culturally? *Remember:* It's important to keep these two in balance. Usually, but not always, culture itself makes certain demands on people. Non-Christians also have certain expectations regarding what is appropriate and what is inappropriate. As Christians we must take into consideration cultural expectations and at the same time not violate biblical principles and teachings. And we still should avoid being legalistic and becoming judgmental of others!

- What are my motives regarding what I wear? Am I attracting attention to myself or to the Lord Jesus Christ who lives within me? *Remember:* You can dress elaborately to attract attention to yourself, or you can be shabby, unkempt, or unclean to attract attention to yourself. Both lead to a lack of respectability.

- What about the house I live in? Did I buy it to impress people or did I buy it to glorify Jesus Christ? *Remember:* This question, as all of these questions, has to be handled individually. Don't judge others. Examine your own heart. Size, cost, and location are not the most important issues; your motives are.

- What about my speech? Do I use words to build up others or to build up myself? Do I glorify God with my words or do I glorify myself? Furthermore, is my speech becoming to a Christian? Does it adorn the doctrine of God?

Listen to Yourself

Reflect on the following illustrations to see what you can learn about yourself.

On one occasion, we were constructing a new building for one of the churches where I served as founding pastor. One of the men on our executive team was a general contractor, and he volunteered to oversee the construction. We also hired another man from the church to do the on-site supervision.

One day the man who oversaw the day-to-day operations came to me expressing deep concern. The general contractor (the man on our executive committee) was using expletives on the job site that were not becoming to any Christian man, let alone one who was in a leadership position in the church. As the senior pastor, I felt responsible to confront the issue. It was a difficult and painful experience for me, because the man chose to resign from his leadership role in the church. What made the experience even more difficult was that this man was also my friend.

TWO DIFFERENT PERSONALITIES

Since that experience, I've discovered other businessmen who publicly claim to be Christians and yet live this kind of dichotomous life. They never use this kind of language around their families or close friends, but once they enter their business environment, they become different personalities. Somehow they justify their language as being necessary to win respect. Sadly, they lose it.

A MARK OF INSECURITY

Frankly, I have concluded that many men use bad language because they're insecure. This becomes their way of covering up their feelings of inferiority. This became particularly obvious to me one day when I was sitting in a graduate-school classroom taking a course in statistics. The professor went to great lengths to scribble extensive and complicated formulas on the chalkboard. The man sitting beside me happened to be rather proficient in statistics. In fact, he was working on his second PhD degree and had shared with me privately that some of the formulas the professor was using weren't accurate. This day, the student could contain himself no longer. He graciously but directly questioned the professor's accuracy.

I'll never forget the verbal explosion that followed. In the twinkling of an eye, the professor's language changed. His expletives were shocking even to a class filled with people who didn't claim to be Christians.

As I reflect on what unfolded that day, it became apparent that my friend had threatened the professor in the worst way. Rather than admitting his error, he tried to cover up his insecurity with bad language. Unfortunately, some Christian men do the same.

INTENSE ANGER

Anger can also cause a man to use bad language. Talk to any professional football player about what happens on the field when tempers flare. Bad language and anger go hand in hand.

Frequently, however, insecurity and anger run on the same track, which leads to double trouble. Insecurity often *causes* anger, which can cause a verbal explosion that is anything but edifying.

Check Yourself

Use the following scriptural exhortations as a checklist to determine the degree of respectability you have with both Christians and non-Christians.

Check those areas where you believe you are particularly strong (√) and mark those areas where you need to improve (X).

YOUR BUSINESS LIFE

☐ But we urge you, brethren, to excel still more, and to make it your ambition to lead a quiet life and attend to your own business and work with your own hands, just as we commanded you, so that you will behave properly toward outsiders and not be in any need (1 Thess. 4:10b–12).

☐ Whatever you do, do your work heartily, as for the Lord rather than for men, knowing that from the Lord you will receive the reward of the inheritance. It is the Lord Christ whom you serve (Col. 3:23–24).

☐ Those who have believers as their masters must not be disrespectful to them because they are brethren, but must serve them all the more, because those who partake of the benefit are believers and beloved (1 Tim. 6:2).

YOUR SOCIAL LIFE

☐ Whether, then, you eat or drink or whatever you do, do all to the glory of God. Give no offense either to Jews or to Greeks or to the church of God; just as I also please all men in all things, not seeking my own profit but the profit of the many, so that they may be saved (1 Cor. 10:31–33).

☐ Conduct yourselves with wisdom toward outsiders, making the most of the opportunity. Let your speech always be with grace, as though seasoned with salt, so that you will know how you should respond to each person (Col. 4:5–6).

☐ Keep your behavior excellent among the Gentiles, so that in the thing in which they slander you as evildoers, they may because of your good deeds, as they observe them, glorify God in the day of visitation (1 Pet. 2:12).

☐ Submit yourselves for the Lord's sake to every human institution, whether to a king as the one in authority, or to governors as sent by him for the punishment of evildoers and the praise of those who do right. For such is the will of God that by doing right you may silence the ignorance of foolish men (vv. 13–15).

YOUR CHURCH LIFE

☐ Only conduct yourselves in a manner worthy of the gospel of Christ, so that whether I come and see you or remain absent, I will hear of you that you are standing firm in one spirit, with one mind striving together for the faith of the gospel (Phil. 1:27).

☐ So then we pursue the things which make for peace and the building up of one another (Rom. 14:19).

☐ Do nothing from selfishness or empty conceit, but with humility of mind regard one another as more important than yourselves; do not merely look out for your own personal interests, but also for the interests of others (Phil. 2:3–4).

☐ But as for you, speak the things which are fitting for sound doctrine (Titus 2:1).

Evaluate

From this study, isolate areas in your life where you need to improve.

Translate those areas into goals and then take action to reach those goals. For example, if you are a person who never gets to work on time, make it your goal to get an early start. Concentrate on this goal until you have developed a new habit.

From this study, pray and ask God to help you achieve those goals.

Realize, however, that prayer alone will not enable you to achieve goals. You must act as a *responsible* human being. As someone once said, we must "put feet to our prayers."

Remember: Bad habits are hard to break, but we must break them if we are to become respectable and to be a good reflection of the life of Jesus Christ.

Thinking and Growing Together

This section is designed for group discussion and personal application after reading and studying the contents of this chapter:

renewal.tv/mm6r

First, make sure someone is appointed to lead the group.

Second, spend time sharing the "greatest learning" from this chapter.

Third, use the following questions for more in-depth discussion.

- What are some personal observations and experiences that help illustrate the importance of developing "respectability"?
- What do you think about the conclusion that some men use bad language because they are insecure or angry?
- What other reasons may cause men to resort to this kind of communication?
- What can we do to become consistent Christians in all areas of our lives? If we have lost respect, how can we regain it?

Set a Goal

Write out one goal you'd like to achieve as a result of this study.

Pray for One Another

Once each man has written out a goal, allow time to share the goals with others and to pray for each other.

Note: No one in the group should feel forced to share or pray. On the other hand, no one should be excluded from participating.

7

Sharing Our Resources

Hospitable
1 Timothy 3:2; Titus 1:8

A Generous Act of Love

A shock wave circled the globe as five missionaries lay dead on the banks of the Curaray River in Ecuador, murdered by savage Auca Indians. The year was 1956. I was a young professor at Moody Bible Institute in Chicago, and I remember that dreadful moment.

A Personal Message from Gene

renewal.tv/mm7i

But I also remember what happened two years later. Rachael Saint, a sister of one of the martyred men, along with Dayuma, a runaway Auca Indian girl, courageously walked back into the tribe under God's guidance and protection. The result has been no less than earth-shattering.

Rachael spent years living among the tribe. Under the auspices of Wycliffe Bible Translators, she learned the language, reduced it to writing, taught the people how to read, and worked to place the completed New Testament in their hands. This saint among savages saw all of her brother's killers convert to Jesus Christ and three of those men became pastors in Auca churches.

During the time Rachael lived among the Auca tribe, she had no running water, bathroom facilities, stove, or conveniences. At the age of 72, she spent two hours a day boiling water, valuable time she could have spent completing her translation work.

I also remember getting word that a crew of nine men from Fellowship Bible Church of San Antonio, an extension of our ministry in Dallas, flew to this remote jungle camp to spend ten days constructing facilities to lighten Rachael's load. The materials for the project were flown into the jungle by Missionary Aviation Fellowship and constructed on-site by these men who personally raised the money to complete the project.

Practicing Hospitality

This story—and many like it—are contemporary illustrations of applying Paul's exhortations in Romans 12:13 (NIV), "Share with the Lord's people who are in need. *Practice hospitality.*"

The word "hospitable" means being generous and caring for others. That is why we call our medical centers "hospitals." They are places where we can help people who are physically and emotionally hurting. However, the *church is also to be a hospital*—not only an environment for spiritual healing, but also a place to meet one another's physical and emotional needs.

It Started in Jerusalem

The circumstances in Jerusalem when the church was founded were, of course, unusual. Thousands of God-fearing Jews had come from throughout the Roman world to worship the Lord for a special fifty-day celebration. On the fiftieth day, the Holy Spirit descended on a small group of believers who were praying in an upper room.

That day, the church was born, and thousands were converted to Jesus Christ. Those who responded to Peter's message included both the God-fearing Hebrews in Jerusalem and Judea as well as the God-fearing Grecian Jews who were visiting the Holy City from all over the Roman world (see Acts 2:5–11 for the various language groups). No one knew what was going to happen next—except that Jesus promised to return. Predictably, the Grecian Jews decided to stay in Jerusalem to see what would happen. At this point, we see the greatest demonstration of hospitality in the history of Christianity. Luke recorded:

> For there was not a needy person among them, for all who were owners of land or houses would sell them and bring the proceeds of the sales and lay them at the apostles' feet, and they would be distributed to each, as any had need. (Acts 4:34–35)

This New Testament example illustrates an ongoing practice throughout Church history. Unusual circumstances will always create special needs among God's people. In New Testament days, it was sometimes a famine, such as the one faced by the Jerusalem Christians several years later. In this instance, the church in Antioch came to the rescue (see Acts 11:25–30). Later, Paul faced special needs because of his imprisonment in Rome, and the Philippian church rose to the occasion (see Phil. 4:10–20).

The Need Is Still with Us

Special needs emerge in the same way today, and when they do, God's people should respond to those needs. In the churches I have pastored, we developed a "love fund" for this purpose—a special account we carefully monitored to make sure it was used to show hospitality. It may also involve using our homes and resources to minister to others, just to share love and friendship.

Paul emphasized the same point in his letter to the Ephesians when he wrote:

He who steals must steal no longer; but rather he must labor, performing with his own hands what is good, so that he may have something to *share with one who has need*. (4:28)

A Willing Spirit

The basis of hospitality is true Christian love. Peter made this point clear when he wrote, "Above all, keep fervent in *your love for one another*, because love covers a multitude of sins" (1 Pet. 4:8). He then followed this powerful admonition by saying,

Be hospitable to one another *without complaint*. (v. 9)

A willing spirit and unselfish motives are the true test of Christian love. We are *not* to respond to others' needs because it is our responsibility or simply a duty. Rather, it is to come from our hearts. We are not to love others for reward, but because God first loved us.

Rewards *will be* granted. You cannot truly reach out to others without eventually receiving. But receiving should not be a part of our basic motivation in demonstrating hospitality.

Saint Francis of Assisi captured this concept of unselfish motives better than anyone I know, even though he probably didn't have a complete understanding of salvation by grace through faith. Nevertheless, he captured what it means to *be hospitable*:

> Lord, make me an instrument of Your peace.
> Where there is hatred let me sow love;
> where there is injury, pardon;
> where there is doubt, faith;
> where there is despair, hope;
> where there is darkness, light;
> where there is sadness, joy.

O Divine Master, grant that I may not so much seek
    to be consoled as to console;
to be understood as to understand;
to be loved as to love.
For it is in giving that we receive;
it is in pardoning that we are pardoned;
and it is in dying that we are born to
eternal life.[1]

A Word of Caution

As Christians, we are told to even "show hospitality to strangers, for by this some have entertained angels without knowing it" (Heb. 13:2). However, we also must be careful. Some people make it a consistent practice to deceive believers and take advantage of their generosity. Through the years, I've experienced this kind of deceit on numerous occasions, and I must admit that I've made some wrong decisions. In short, I've been taken.

One day, I was sitting in my favorite doughnut shop. Next to me was a woman my wife and I had tried to befriend. Her life had been a disaster. She was divorced and had several children. Her comments made it clear she had been "sleeping" with guys she had met.

As I came into the doughnut shop that morning, I sat down beside her and began to plan my day. At first, we exchanged hellos as we normally did, and then I went about my business.

Several minutes later, she leaned over and quietly asked me if I could lend her twenty dollars to fill her car with gas. "I'll pay it back," she said, "as soon as I get my next paycheck."

I'm a compassionate person at heart, so I reached for my billfold. I then realized I had only enough money with me to pay for a doughnut and a cup of coffee. "I'm sorry," I said. "I don't have any money except enough to pay my bill, but if I did, I'd help you out."

I probably would have given her the money, and I probably would never have gotten the money back. That, of course, would not have been a disaster, but had I helped her, it probably would have only reinforced her irresponsibility.

Later, when I was a little more objective, I thought about several things. First, she always had enough money for cigarettes. She was a chain-smoker. Second, she commented later in our conversation that she should have been at work, but was running late, and she didn't seem to care much. She continued to sit at the counter, smoke up a storm, eat doughnuts, and drink coffee. And third, I thought, *I know I'm supposed to show hospitality because I might be entertaining an angel unawares, but this girl ain't no angel.*

Determining True Need

The writer of Hebrews is not teaching us that we should be indiscreet and respond to everybody who asks for a handout. Some people are irresponsible and downright manipulative. It would not be the loving thing to do to enable them to continue this kind of behavior. This is why we should be cautious and develop sensitive systems to determine true needs and if people are trustworthy.

However, the cumulative teaching of the Bible is that we should care about those in real need, including people we don't know. By sharing only a cup of cold water, we are sharing with Jesus Christ Himself (see Mark 9:41). As Christ-followers, we are to be generous and hospitable. This is one of the outstanding marks of Christian maturity and this is why Paul lists hospitality as one of the positive qualities in his letter to Timothy and in his letter to Titus (see 1:8). It reflects Christian maturity and helps us to develop good reputations.

Hospitality Begins at Home

The overall teaching from Scripture regarding the quality of hospitality as a sign of maturity definitely focuses on the way we use our homes. This was particularly true in the New Testament world. Believers had no permanent place to meet except in homes. If a man became a spiritual leader, chances are the church would meet in his home. How could he be qualified as a spiritual leader without being generous in the area of hospitality?

Showing hospitality is a mark of maturity in any Christian man. True, our economic circumstances influence how much we are able to do. The size of our homes makes a difference in the number of people we can entertain. But on the other hand, in the churches I've pastored, I have seen people with small homes and apartments demonstrate hospitality just as often as people who have large homes. True Christian love transcends economic status. And when it does not, it should. That is why James wrote:

> But the brother of humble circumstances is to glory in his high position; and the rich man is to glory in his humiliation, because like flowering grass he will pass away. (1:9–10)

Points of Action

The following projects are designed to help you develop the quality of hospitality.

Love Is the Key

Demonstrating Christ-like love is foundational in developing the quality of hospitality. Almost every passage in the New Testament that refers to this characteristic is encased in a context that emphasizes Christian love. Note the following references:

☐ *Let love be without hypocrisy*. Abhor what is evil; cling to what is good. *Be devoted to one another in brotherly love;* give preference to one another in honor; not lagging behind in diligence, fervent in spirit, serving the Lord; rejoicing in hope, persevering in tribulation, devoted to prayer, contributing to the needs of the saints, practicing *hospitality* (Rom. 12:9–13).

☐ Above all, *keep fervent in your love for one another*, because *love* covers a multitude of sins. Be *hospitable* to one another without complaint (1 Pet. 4:8–9).

☐ *Let love of the brethren continue.* Do not neglect to show *hospitality* to strangers, for by this some have entertained angels without knowing it (Heb. 13:1–2).

Remember: Biblical love *is not just a feeling.* It is an attitude and involves action. Christian love is patience, kindness, generosity, humility, courtesy, unselfishness, good temper, guilelessness, and sincerity (see 1 Cor. 13:4–7).[2]

Love Is Doing What Is Right

Some people wait for a *desire* to show hospitality. This may never come. You may need to start showing hospitality before you begin to sense any reward whatsoever at the feeling level.

Let's face it. Thinking about showing hospitality may threaten us. But we must remember that "perfect love casts out fear" (1 John 4:18). As we begin to practice biblical love, fear and threat will begin to subside.

Develop a Plan

Decide on some specific ways to show hospitality:

- Look for opportunities to share your home with spiritual leaders—pastors, missionaries, and other Christian workers. Invite them for dinner or to stay in your home.
- Look for opportunities to share your home with other members of the body of Christ who comprise your own local church.

    Remember: A special physical need is not necessary for you to show hospitality. The need might be social, emotional, or spiritual. Many Christians are lonely and in need of fellowship, and may be too bashful to reach out to others. They are waiting for an invitation to share their lives with someone else.

> **Begin to show hospitality no matter how you feel about it.**

- Show hospitality to non-Christians by beginning with the people around you: your neighbor across the street or the person who works beside you at your job.

Remember: You are the Christian. You are the one who should be reaching out. Invite these people to dinner or ask them to join you in an evening of relaxation and social activity.

A *word of caution:* Don't get overly ambitious. Begin by building friendships with one or two non-Christians. Frequently this will set the stage for an invitation to a Bible class in your home or for you to personally share the Gospel of Jesus Christ.

- Open your home for an informal Bible study, either for Christians or non-Christians.

Remember: To invite non-Christians to your home for a Bible study means building friendships first. We must learn to love people because they are people and not just because we want to win them to Christ.

Thinking and Growing Together

This section is designed for group discussion and personal application after reading and studying the contents of this chapter:

Suggestions for Discussion and Application

renewal.tv/mm7r

First, make sure someone is appointed to lead the group.

Second, spend time sharing the "greatest learning" from this chapter.

Third, use the following questions for more in-depth discussion.

- Why do we hesitate to practice hospitality as we should?
- What can we do to overcome the barriers that keep us from practicing hospitality?
- Can you think of something you'd like to do immediately to begin to develop this spiritual quality in your life? Would you mind sharing it with us?
- What are some of the things you're already doing to show hospitality?

Set a Goal

Write out one goal you'd like to achieve as a result of this study.

_____

_____

_____

_____

_____

_____

Pray for One Another

Once each man has written out a goal, allow time to share the goals with others and to pray for each other.

Note: No one in the group should feel forced to share or pray. On the other hand, no one should be excluded from participating.

8

Communicating Sensitively

Able to teach

1 Timothy 3:2

A Definite Setup!

I have a close friend who was involved in the banking industry for years. At one point Mike served as CEO of one of the largest savings and loan organizations in the state of Texas.

A Personal Message from Gene

renewal.tv/mm8i

One Saturday morning, he and his wife, Sharon, had an unusual experience. They were sitting at home having a quiet breakfast. Hearing some commotion, they looked out their front window and saw a group of people get off a bus and then begin to picket their house.

In a few minutes, a man holding a document knocked on the front door. This total stranger wanted Mike to sign the document confessing that his savings and loan organization was "redlining" minorities. Standing beside him was another man holding a camera, obviously ready to take a picture of Mike and his reaction.

The fact is that the government *had* passed legislation that could give this impression. Since First Texas Savings and Loan was prominent in the state of Texas, and since Mike was CEO, they targeted him in order to let the government know they were not happy.

Mike quickly perceived that this was a setup. These people never expected to get his signature but, rather, an argument or a slammed door. Reading between the lines, this would look great on the front page of the *Dallas Morning News* the next day, and hence the man with the camera.

An Unexpected Invitation

These men got neither an argument nor a slammed door. Rather, Mike invited them—and all the picketers—to come into his family room for a cup of coffee and an open discussion. As these people huddled on the front lawn, they at first couldn't believe what was happening. However, they knew this invitation was sincere. Consequently, they laid down their placards and one by one entered Mike's family room.

While Sharon served them coffee, Mike began to share his own journey as a long-term resident in Dallas. He told them of his concerns for minorities as well as some of his own efforts in helping overcome inappropriate attitudes and actions.

A Ministry Moment

At the right moment, the Holy Spirit enabled Mike to share an important event in his own life that forever changed his perspective on others. He told his visitors of his conversion to Christ in a Bible study in the home of one of his neighbors. At that point, mouths began to drop open, and Mike even began to get some positive affirmations. Apparently, some in the group at least understood the gospel.

To make a long story short, these picketers eventually left, each one thanking Mike and Sharon for their hospitality. Not another word was ever mentioned about their grievances. They got on the bus and drove away, and Mike never heard from them again.

A Marvelous Example

I heard Mike share this story at one of our elder/pastor retreats. I immediately thought of the quality of being "able to teach," which Paul listed in both of his letters to Timothy. In the first letter—as we've noted—this quality of maturity is simply listed. However, in his second letter Paul used the concept more definitively.

Once Mike sat down, I stood up and shared the passage from 2 Timothy to demonstrate how Mike had fleshed out in his life that Saturday morning what Paul had written:

> But refuse foolish and ignorant speculations, knowing that they produce *quarrels*. The Lord's bond-servant must not be *quarrelsome*, but be *kind* to all, *able to teach, patient* when wronged, with *gentleness* correcting those who are in opposition, if perhaps God may grant them repentance leading to the knowledge of the truth. (2 Tim. 2:23–25)

What would you have done if you had been in Mike's shoes? Frankly, I would have probably triggered an argument, falling into the trap that had been set. After all, these people would have invaded my space. This was *my* home. They were on private property. And to make matters worse, they were accusing me falsely.

But that's not the way Mike reacted. He attempted to "get inside" the minds and hearts of these people and to understand their grievances. He didn't go on the defensive. He was "kind to all" by inviting them into his home. He was "patient when wronged" even though he was being accused falsely. He corrected with "gentleness."

In short, Mike was "able to teach." Consequently many in this group of adverse people changed their attitudes. Most importantly, many clearly heard Mike's testimony regarding his relationship with Jesus Christ and how it changed his life. Hopefully, some of them not only came to a "knowledge of the truth" regarding Mike's concern for minorities, but to an understanding of what Jesus meant when He said, "I am . . . the truth" (John 14:6).

Didaktikos

The little phrase "able to teach," which Paul used to describe maturity, is a powerful concept. It comes from one Greek word, *didaktikos*, and though there are hundreds of references in the New Testament that refer to some form of teaching, this particular word is used only twice and is translated "able to teach."

Our natural tendency is to interpret this phrase "able to teach" through our own experiential grid. We think of good teachers we have known through the years, people who are effective communicators and who skillfully motivate people to learn. We might think of high-powered lecturers who have held us spellbound. In actuality, we are thinking about their abilities, skills, and expertise.

A Powerful Cluster of Words

The fact is that *didaktikos* has a far broader meaning than just pedagogical skill. You can see this clearly when you look at how Paul used the word in his second letter to Timothy. Note that the English phrase "able to teach" is surrounded by words that describe not skills but *qualities of life*. In his communication, Timothy was to avoid *arguments*. He was to be *kind* to all people—Christians and non-Christians. He was to be *patient* even when falsely accused and personally attacked. He was to correct those who opposed him in a *gentle* manner. And sandwiched right in the middle of these qualities of life is the phrase "able to teach."

Clearly, to be *able to teach* means that we must learn how to communicate with others in a nonthreatening, nondefensive manner. We are to avoid arguments by being sensitive to people who are confused or even obstinate. When verbally abused, we don't respond in the same way. In short, a man who is *able to teach* is a person who is not in bondage to himself. Rather, his true identity in Jesus Christ has enabled him to be in control of his mind and emotions.

> A man who is able to teach is a person who is not in bondage to himself.

A Personal Confession

I remember one experience as a young Bible college teacher in which I didn't demonstrate this quality well. A student who was several years older than I persistently disagreed with me in one of the classes I was teaching. He became obnoxious. One day I became so infuriated—and threatened—with his behavior that I gathered up my lecture notes, dismissed the class, and walked out the door, leaving the students to fend for themselves.

Later, I found out why this man tried so hard to intimidate me. He came to my office one day and explained why he had tried to embarrass me. He then asked for forgiveness. You see, I had begun dating a girl on campus, who is now my wife. He confessed that he had his eye on Elaine, but I had "beat him to the draw." I, of course, was completely unaware of his intentions and feelings. Once he unraveled his story, it all made sense. I certainly forgave him, and I asked forgiveness for not reflecting more maturity myself. If I had been more experienced, I could have handled the situation much differently.

In hindsight, I should have asked the student to see me personally after class to discuss his concerns. I would have looked for the real reason for his attitudes and actions. Had I done this, I could have demonstrated more Christlikeness to the students—that I was really *able to teach* in the full sense of what the phrase means.

That experience taught me a great lesson. I've been able to handle similar situations in a much more godly fashion and with God's help have been able to communicate nondefensively in some very difficult circumstances.

Our Attitude toward Scripture

Consider another significant dimension to the meaning of being "able to teach." Although Paul does not use the word *didaktikos* in his letter to Titus, he made several statements that refer to the same concept. He wrote that a mature man is "*self-controlled,* holding fast the faithful word which is in accordance with the teaching, so that he will be able both *to exhort* in sound doctrine and *to refute* those who contradict" (Titus 1:8–9).

Here Paul demonstrated that being "able to teach" doesn't mean we compromise the Word of God. A mature man of God is to hold fast to the faithful word. But at the same time, he does not allow himself to get involved in "foolish and ignorant speculations" (2 Tim. 2:23). Again, we see a significant correlation between Paul's comments to Timothy and his comments to Titus.

Our Understanding of Scripture

A man who is *able to teach* not only is self-controlled and convinced that the Word of God is true, but also understands the Scriptures sufficiently to be "able both to exhort in sound doctrine and to refute those who contradict" (Titus 1:9). We cannot communicate God's truth without knowledge of the Word of God. This is why Paul also wrote to Timothy:

The things which you have heard from me in the presence of many witnesses, entrust these to faithful men who will be *able to teach others also*. (2 Tim. 2:2)

As maturing Christian men, we must constantly be learning more and more of God's Word, and understanding it. Only then can we teach it. This is why Paul also wrote the following words to Timothy:

Be diligent to present yourself approved to God as a workman who does not need to be ashamed, *accurately handling the word of truth*. (v. 15)

To Sum Up

A man who is "able to teach" demonstrates three significant qualities:

First, he must be characterized by spiritual and emotional maturity—being able to handle himself in threatening situations.

Second, he has a firm conviction that the Word of God is true.

Third, he understands the Word of God sufficiently to be able to communicate it to others.

Points of Action

The following project is designed to help all of us develop the quality of being *able to teach*.

- It's essential in being a good father. Paul underscored this when he wrote to the Ephesians:

    Fathers, do not provoke your children to anger, but bring them up in the discipline and instruction of the Lord. (6:4)

- This quality is also essential for being a participating member of your local church. Paul underscored this point in his letter to the Colossians:

> Let the word of Christ richly dwell within you, with all wisdom *teaching and admonishing one another* with psalms and hymns and spiritual songs, singing with thankfulness in your hearts to God. (3:16)

- This quality is related to our understanding of Scripture. This is why it's essential to be involved in a program of Bible study, preferably in a group. This provides accountability, which we all need. Furthermore, learning Scripture together in community is a biblical principle, and every member of the group can contribute to the learning process. Clearly the Holy Spirit uses this dynamic within the body of Christ (see Eph. 4:16).

- This quality is related to our emotional maturity. Consequently, all of us should develop psychologically so we'll not be threatened when discussing the Word of God with those who may disagree with us. But remember that a mere knowledge of Scripture will not automatically solve this kind of personality problem. There are many people who know the Bible from cover to cover but they become defensive and highly threatened when someone challenges their interpretation of Scripture. If we're not careful, we can use the Bible as a personal sword rather than as the sword of the Spirit.

The Life Essentials Study Bible

Many years after I first penned this book, the Lord gave me the opportunity to create a study Bible, the *Life Essentials Study Bible*. The invitation came as a surprise at the time I was passing the baton of leadership to my successor in the last church I pastored in the Dallas area (initially called Fellowship Bible Church North but now called Chase Oaks Church). Using the *Holman Christian Standard Bible* translation, I embedded in the biblical text 1,500

"Principles to Live By" from Genesis to Revelation. I included with each life principle a brief commentary followed by a question for application, which I called "Reflection and Response."

In addition, each of the 1,500 principles has a QR code printed in the Bible which enables the reader to access 1,500 videos that were recorded as I taught these 1,500 principles to a live audience.

Thankfully this has become a great resource both for personal and small group study. For example, one group of men I know personally each watch the videos before they meet to discuss the "Reflection and Response" questions. Another group comes together and then watches the videos and uses my presentations as a basis for their interaction and application. These are just two illustrations of how the Bible can be used for group study and accountability. (For more information on the *Life Essentials Study Bible*, go to www .bibleprinciples.org.)

> Teaching involves more than working with a group; it is also a one-on-one process.

Note: You can use the QR codes and my video presentations in the same way with this study on Christian maturity.

Becoming "Able to Teach"

The following are some practical suggestions for developing this quality of life:

- If someone attacks you personally, never retaliate out of threat or embarrassment. Respond warmly and with openness. Draw them out even more.

  Remember: "A gentle answer turns away wrath, but a harsh word stirs up anger" (Prov. 15:1).

- If you are too emotional at the moment to respond objectively, it's better to refrain from commenting until you have developed a degree of objectivity and emotional control.

To help you achieve this goal, memorize and practice the words of James:

> This you know, my beloved brethren. But everyone must be *quick to hear, slow to speak* and *slow to anger;* for the anger of man does not achieve the righteousness of God. (1:19–20)

- Try not to embarrass people publicly, even though they may attack you publicly. If you want to reduce the tension in a group setting, seek to speak to those who disagree in a private setting. This is also true when disciplining children.
- If you continue to have problems with insecurity and feelings of threat, seek out a mature Christian friend or counselor. Attempt to understand the reasons for your defensiveness. Be open and honest about your feelings and why you believe this happens.
- Gently force yourself to function in threatening situations. This is difficult but necessary. You will develop confidence as you begin to act and succeed in your communication.

   Warning: Don't run away when you fail. Learn from the failure.

   Remember: The more you succeed, the more confidence you'll develop.

Thinking and Growing Together

This section is designed for group discussion and personal application after reading and studying the contents of this chapter:

Suggestions for Discussion and Application

renewal.tv/mm8r

First, make sure someone is appointed to lead the group.

Second, spend time sharing the "greatest learning" from this chapter.

Third, use the following questions for more in-depth discussion.

- What communication experiences have you had that were threatening? How did you handle them?
- Who are some of your favorite teachers who model the true meaning of being able to teach? Why?
- Describe some communication experiences you wish you could do over again.
- Describe a communication experience—either positive or negative—in which you learned your greatest lesson.

Set a Goal

Write out one goal you'd like to achieve as a result of this study.

_____

_____

_____

_____

_____

_____

_____

Pray for One Another

Once each man has written out a goal, allow time to share the goals with others and to pray for each other.

Note: No one in the group should feel forced to share or pray. On the other hand, no one should be excluded from participating.

9

Being Moderate in All Things

Not addicted to wine

1 Timothy 3:3

An Irate Mother

Several years ago, I received a letter from a mother whose teenage son was drinking more than Coca-Cola and orange juice. Knowing her concerns, someone recommended that she give her son a copy of my book *The Measure of a Man*. She thought it was a good idea but decided to read the book herself before giving it to her son—which is certainly commendable. However, when she got to this chapter on moderation, she became extremely angry, tore up the book, and threw it in the trash can. She then wrote me, told me what she had done, accused me of false teaching, and condemned me for perverting the Word of God and leading people astray. You see, I had pointed out in this chapter that the Bible doesn't teach total abstinence per se.

A Personal Message from Gene

renewal.tv/mm9i

Winning Battles and Losing Wars

Personal attacks are not pleasant experiences. But frankly, this woman's letter saddened me. I could see that she might have been trying to "win a battle," but she might very well "lose the war" with her son. The fact is that the Bible *does not teach total abstinence*—though it does teach that total abstinence might be a very important decision.

Merrill Unger reminds us that in most of the passages of the Old Testament where the common word for wine is used, the reference "certainly means fermented grape juice."[1] The same is true in the New Testament. There is no way to prove that references to wine were to only nonalcoholic grape juice. Rather, all historical, cultural, and exegetical evidence points in the opposite direction.

To be true to Scripture, we must also interpret Paul's references to wine in his letters to Timothy and Titus in the same way. Paul was not stating that a mature man of God should never *partake* of wine. Rather, he was not to be *addicted* to it (1 Tim. 3:3; Titus 1:7).

What the Bible Teaches

Drunkenness Is Definitely Condemned

Both the Old and New Testaments clearly teach against drunkenness. In Proverbs we read:

> Do not be with heavy drinkers of wine, or with gluttonous eaters of meat; for the heavy drinker and the glutton will come to poverty, and drowsiness will clothe one with rags. (23:20–21)

Later in the same chapter of Proverbs, we discover a series of questions:

- Who has woe?
- Who has sorrow?

- Who has contentions?
- Who has complaining?
- Who has wounds without cause?
- Who has redness of eyes? (v. 29).

We then find the answer to these questions:

> Those who linger long over wine, those who go to taste mixed wine. (v. 30)

A serious warning follows this explicit explanation regarding the price people pay when they overindulge:

> Do not look on the wine when it is red, when it sparkles in the cup, when it goes down smoothly; at the last it bites like a serpent, and stings like a viper. Your eyes will see strange things, and your mind will utter perverse things. (vv. 31–33)

The New Testament writers are just as clear in their teaching. Paul wrote to the Ephesians:

> And do not get drunk with wine, for that is dissipation, but be filled with the Spirit. (5:18)

Addictive Behavior Is Sinful

Addictive behavior was Paul's primary concern in his letters to Timothy and Titus when he outlined a profile for Christian maturity. He wrote to the Corinthians: "All things are lawful for me, but not all things are profitable. All things are lawful for me, but I will not be *mastered by anything*" (1 Cor. 6:12).

We can become enslaved even to those things that are not wrong in themselves.

Here Paul was not condoning sinful behavior when he said—"all things are lawful for me." Rather, he was saying that we can become enslaved even to those things that are not wrong in themselves, such as food and the fruit of the vine. In terms of wine, some people drink and get drunk; but some also become addicted. They *consistently* overindulge. Today, we classify these people as alcoholics.

Alcohol addiction is a significant problem in today's culture. This is why some people believe in total abstinence, and rightfully so for alcoholics or even for those who have this propensity. But it's *not* accurate to say that the Bible teaches that *all Christians* should abstain from drinking wine.

We Are to Avoid Being a Stumbling Block

The Bible also teaches that we should never cause anyone to stumble and fall into sin. Paul made this point clear in his letter to the Romans:

> It is good not to *eat meat* or to *drink wine*, or to *do anything* by which your brother stumbles. (14:21)

Children of alcoholics run a four times greater risk of becoming alcoholics than children of nonalcoholics.[2] True, we can engage in the age-old argument regarding what causes these kinds of problems—heredity or the environment—but both are involved. Even though genetic factors can play a significant role in the development of alcoholism, it is still true that *modeling* plays a great part in causing children to start drinking. When children have a propensity to become addicted, they move more easily in that direction by parental examples. Children will often do what we do, not necessarily what we say they should do.

Yet the issue is far greater than having children who exhibit a natural inclination toward alcoholism, either psychologically or physically or both. Although we, as their parents, may be moderate drinkers, our children live in an alcoholic society. They experience incredible peer pressures. Social acceptance is a tremendous force, and even children who have good parental models can be led astray. Consider what happens on college campuses!

We Are Not to Judge One Another

Within a period of two weeks, two men in the church I pastored approached me regarding drinking wine. They were well aware of the problems in our society and knew the dangers of alcoholism. But the factor that triggered their question that day related to their children. Was it worth the risk to drink, although moderate drinking was not a sin for them? Would their freedom in Christ eventually cause one of their children to abuse this freedom?

As we discussed the matter, they both came to the conclusion that drinking alcohol in front of their children was not worth the risk. One decided on total abstinence. The other decided on abstinence in front of the children. Both made decisions based on principles of Scripture (see Rom. 14).

Avoid Other Overindulgences

Overeating

Eating and *drinking* are often mentioned together in the Bible. Let's face it! There are Christians who overeat regularly but would never touch a drop of alcohol. Unfortunately, some of these Christians are the most vociferous in condemning users of alcohol. Yet, they are consistently overweight, not because of glandular problems—which is another issue—but because of a lack of self-discipline.

Jesus Christ had some strong words to say about this kind of judgmental behavior:

> And why do you look at the speck that is in your brother's eye, but do not notice the log that is in your own eye? Or how can you say to your brother, 'Let me take the speck out of your eye,' and

behold, the log is in your own eye? You hypocrite, first take the log out of your own eye, and then you will see clearly to take the speck out of your brother's eye. (Matt. 7:3–5)

Smoking

We cannot deny the harmful effects that smoking has on our bodies. Consider the following observations I made after reading several online resources:

- Cigarette smoking is a major cause of emphysema, chronic bronchitis, lung cancer, and heart disease.[3]
- Pregnant women who smoke have more spontaneous abortions, premature births, and low weight births than women who do not smoke.[4]
- In 2014, almost 10 percent of high school students were current cigarette smokers.[5]
- We're told that 443,000 people die yearly from diseases associated with smoking or secondhand smoke.[6]
- If people never smoked, 80 percent of lung cancer deaths would be avoided.[7]

These observations speak for themselves. As Christians, we should do nothing that will interfere with our health. Again, we must remember that the Holy Spirit dwells within us, and He wants to use our bodies to glorify Jesus Christ and to carry out His purposes on this earth.

Maintaining Our Christian Witness

One day I had a conversation with a woman who was trying to witness to the people in her office by letting them know that as a Christian she didn't drink alcohol. She appeared surprised when I shared with her that she need not make this an issue. People knew her preference simply by her actions. Neither did she have to drink to win a listening ear. In our culture, people generally respect others who refuse alcoholic beverages. A simple "no, thank you" is all we have to say. We can graciously refuse a drink and then concentrate on building relationships with non-Christian co-workers, looking for opportunities to share the gospel, which is based not on our commitment to total abstinence but on our relationship with the Lord Jesus Christ.

Actions Speak Louder Than Words

While staying in a motel in Denver, Colorado, I had some free time and decided to work on my Sunday message. As I often do, I went to a restaurant nearby to get a cup of coffee and to continue my research. Because it was dinnertime, they hesitated to seat me in the main dining room and suggested that I go to the bar.

Imagine the scene! There I was reading my Bible and drinking a cup of coffee. Ironically, I was studying what the Scriptures had to say about the subject of not being "addicted to wine."

Seated behind me were two couples who very obviously glanced my way. I overheard a bit of their conversation, and it was apparent they were intrigued that I was studying my Bible in a bar. Finally, one of them mustered up enough courage to ask me what I was doing. To their amazement, they found out I was a pastor preparing a message for the weekend. But they also commented jokingly that I was *only* drinking coffee.

> The Bible clearly teaches that Christians should never partake of anything that harms their bodies, clouds their thinking, or brings them into bondage.

I was rather amused that they thought my Bible and the bar didn't mix. I could sense that the very presence of the Word of God made them feel somewhat uncomfortable. However, the fact that I was at ease opened the door to be a Christian witness.

Though this has been the only time I have studied my Bible in a bar, in this instance it seemed to be an opportune moment.

Points of Action

The following project is designed to help you develop a Christian lifestyle that conforms to biblical principles.

Don't Judge Others

You may consider yourself a mature Christian, having developed certain boundaries for your own life. However, have you made absolute for other Christians what God has created to be a freedom? For example, God has given you the freedom to abstain from drinking any alcoholic beverage. But God has also given other Christians freedom to partake, although as has been shown, He has set definite boundaries.

On the other hand, perhaps God has given you freedom to drink moderately. Are you judging those who have decided on abstinence? As Paul wrote, "Each person must be fully convinced in his own mind" (Rom. 14:5).

Practice the Higher Principle

Although Paul did not teach abstinence, and although he instructed Timothy to "use a little wine" (1 Tim. 5:23) for health reasons, he also told the Romans, "It is good not to eat meat or to drink wine, or to do anything *by which your brother stumbles*" (Rom. 14:21). The issue Paul was concerned about in Romans 14 was not the meat or the wine per se. Rather, it was the idolatrous associations and the problems partaking may have created for weak Christians. As Paul wrote to the Corinthians, "Some people are still so accustomed to idols that when they eat sacrificial food they think of it as having been sacrificed to an idol, and since their conscience is weak, it is defiled" (1 Cor. 8:7 NIV).

Furthermore, these New Testament believers had at one time engaged in sexual orgies associated with drinking wine and gluttonous behavior. Consequently, when they returned to the temple to buy food, some of them were so weak and immature spiritually that they regressed to this sinful and immoral behavior.

Paul was saying that at times abstinence is the better way to live. *Love and concern for others is the higher principle,* and mature, sensitive Christians are willing to avoid certain activities, although they may be legitimate in themselves. Does anything in your life violate this broader and higher principle?

Be Disciplined

The Bible clearly teaches that Christians should never partake of *anything* that harms their bodies, clouds their thinking, or brings them into bondage. If you believe you lack discipline in any area in your life, the following specific suggestions will help you:

- Isolate the problem.
- Discuss the problem with several other mature Christians to see if they concur that it is a serious issue or just an oversensitive conscience.
- If others concur that the problem is real, ask them to pray regularly for you.
- Write out the problem and then set a specific goal you wish to accomplish in overcoming the problem. Read your goal several times a day if necessary.
- Develop a regular time to study the Scriptures and to meditate and pray about the problem.

    Remember: Many Christians fail consistently because they are programmed for failure. If you want to overcome a problem, program yourself for victory in Jesus Christ.

Pastoral and Professional Help

If you cannot overcome your difficulty by following these suggestions, seek help from a competent Christian counselor. It may be that you need to come to grips with some deeper roots that are causing this problem. For example, overdrinking and overeating are frequently a reflection of emotional issues such as fear, anxiety, insecurity, and anger. It's common knowledge that many alcoholics and food addicts are engaging in these behaviors to medicate themselves—particularly against emotional pain. If this is true, you may need professional help to assist you in understanding these issues, and you'll definitely need a support group to encourage you and to hold you accountable. All of us need encouragement from other members of the body of Christ, but people with addictions need this support on a regular basis.

Thinking and Growing Together

This section is designed for group discussion and personal application after reading and studying the contents of this chapter:

Suggestions for Discussion and Application

First, make sure someone is appointed to lead the group.

Second, spend time sharing the "greatest learning" from this chapter.

renewal.tv/mm9r

Third, use the following questions for more in-depth discussion.

- Do you agree or disagree with the guidelines in this chapter? Why or why not?
- What personal experiences can you share that verify the importance of following these biblical guidelines?

- How can a Christian avoid judging others in the area of drinking alcoholic beverages? How can this be done in other areas involving Christian liberty?
- How can Christians avoid using their Christian liberty in ways that cause others to stumble and fall into sin?
- How can Christians avoid rationalizing engaging in behaviors that may indeed be sinful?

Set a Goal

Write out one goal you'd like to achieve as a result of this study.

_____

_____

_____

_____

_____

_____

_____

Pray for One Another

Once each man has written out a goal, allow time to share the goals with others and to pray for each other.

Note: No one in the group should feel forced to share or pray. On the other hand, no one should be excluded from participating.

10

Overcoming Self-Centeredness

Not self-willed

Titus 1:7

Rubbing Others the Wrong Way

During my single years in ministry, I had a very self-centered roommate. Everyone who had a close relationship with this young man came to this same conclusion. In fact, almost everyone who knew I shared a room with him felt sorry for me.

A Personal Message from Gene

renewal.tv/mm10i

I did my best to make this relationship work. Yet the more I gave in to my roommate's whims and wishes, and the more I tolerated his irritating behavior, the more he seemed to take advantage of me.

As we sat together talking one evening, his actions pushed me over the edge. All the resentment and frustration I had allowed to

117

build within me for many months came pouring out. I told him not only how I felt but also how everyone else felt.

Fortunately, God used this confrontation to get his attention. As I shared my frustration and deep feelings of hurt and anxiety, I literally wept. Although I certainly could have improved my method of communication that day, God used it nevertheless. Somehow my roommate saw beyond my frustration and anger to my personal concern for his welfare and his reputation as a Christian. Furthermore, he knew in his heart that I had patiently put up with a lot of self-oriented behavior on his part.

Although he didn't verbally acknowledge that what I shared was true, he immediately made some changes. He began to be more sensitive and others-oriented. I could tell that he was attempting to make some midcourse corrections in his life.

> A Christian man who is self-centered, self-pleasing, and self-oriented does not have a good reputation.

Shortly after that confrontation, he moved on to another ministry. My greatest reward, however, came several years later. He wrote me a letter and acknowledged that most everything I had said that day was accurate. He wanted me to know that while I was pointing out these things to him, he knew *then* that it was true. However, at that moment, he couldn't bring himself to admit it. He wanted me to know he had changed.

What Others Think

I share this story not to put my friend down or to make myself look good, for I had my own share of immaturity. My purpose is to illustrate that any professing Christian man who is self-centered, self-pleasing, and self-oriented does not have a good reputation. He is overbearing and frequently rubs others the wrong way.

The Greek word *authadees* can be translated "self-willed" in Titus 1:7, and is used in only one other place in the New Testament—in Peter's second epistle. Here the apostle warned Christians against false teachers and how to recognize them. They "will follow their sensuality . . . and in their greed they will exploit you with false words" (2:2–3). They "despise authority" and are "daring" and "*self-willed*" (v. 10). Their hearts are "trained in greed" (v. 14), and they speak with "arrogant words of vanity" (v. 18).

Peter was describing an extreme manifestation of this negative characteristic. But any self-willed man is a self-centered man. He is his own authority. He is often greedy and vain.

Joseph H. Thayer has defined this characteristic as self-pleasing and arrogant.[1] In essence, a self-willed man builds the world around himself. He wants to "do as he pleases."[2] Williams translates that a man who is *not* self-willed is "not stubborn."[3]

That's Not Me!

Because Peter used the word "self-willed" to describe a person whose arrogance and self-centeredness were blasphemous and horribly sinful, it's easy to rationalize. The fact is that we may be appalled at what Peter described but still be *self-oriented*. We have simply sugarcoated our sinful behavior with regular church and Bible study attendance and with religious language. In other words, we may have strong biblical beliefs and yet be guilty of failure in this area of our lives. Although our basic doctrines—what we believe about God, Jesus Christ, the Holy Spirit, and how to be saved—may be correct, we may still be arrogant and self-willed. We are still reflecting "the deeds of the flesh" (Gal. 5:19), or as the AMP reads, "The practices of the sinful nature" rather than "the fruit of the Spirit" (vv. 19, 22).

The Self-Willed Continuum

Self-centeredness comes in various degrees. If we're not on guard, any one of us can fall into this trap. It's easy to be self-pleasing and overbearing. But at some point this kind of behavior breeds resentment, lack of respect, and lack of trust. If we persistently demonstrate this trait, people will not feel comfortable around us or respect us. It affects our reputation.

Why We Avoid Confronting the Self-Willed Person

It's difficult to confront a self-willed Christian because "teachability" is not that person's strong suit. Most of us resist telling such a person our true feelings because we're intimidated and often fear rejection. Rather, we're tempted to work hard to please and to be accepted by an overbearing person. Unfortunately, people naturally talk *about* this person rather than *to* this person. This was certainly true in my experience that I shared at the beginning of this chapter.

Marital Relationships

Nothing is more devastating to a marriage than a self-oriented spouse. Selfishness probably destroys more relationships than any other negative characteristic. Although both husbands and wives can be guilty of being self-centered, as men we're particularly vulnerable—and there are reasons!

First, our egos are easily threatened, which is one of our greatest weaknesses. This can quickly lead to selfish actions. And if we're honest with others and ourselves, we'll admit this is often a smoke screen to cover up our feelings of insecurity and a weak self-image.

Second, as men we tend to operate at a *rational level* more than at a *feeling level*. Consequently, we often don't understand how our overbearing approach to leadership affects our wives. When they try to tell us how they feel, rather than listening, we give them ten reasons why they shouldn't feel that way.

If we are honest, we know we often respond to our wives with logic because we are threatened by their negative feelings. We are not only trying to prove to them that they shouldn't feel the way they feel, but we're also trying to prove to ourselves that we are not to blame for their feelings.

In some respects, I found it easier to reflect Christ's love when I was single than when I got married. Having to relate to my wife 24/7 is far more demanding than having to relate to my friends, my fellow Christians, and the larger Christian community. To love my Christian neighbors as Christ loved me is one thing. But to love my wife as Christ loved the church is yet another.

This is why Paul emphasized this point for husbands in his letters to the Ephesians and Colossians:

Husbands, love your wives, just as Christ also loved the church and gave Himself up for her. (Eph. 5:25)

Husbands, love your wives, and do not be embittered against them. (Col. 3:19)

Paul knew that marriage puts far greater demands on our commitment to Christ. Not only do we become more aware of our own selfish tendencies, but we are also faced with the challenge of living with our mate's weaknesses.

The truth is that no husband is perfect and no wife is perfect. Unless we are truly committed to practicing God's principles of love, our imperfections are likely to create alienation rather than mutual Christian growth and edification as God intended—and increased intimacy.

Parent-Child Relationships

Our ability to be humble and kind is tested even further in our relationships with our children. A self-willed father can devastate and discourage his children. Though this is true for both parents, it is particularly applicable to fathers, which is why Paul wrote:

> *Fathers*, do not provoke your children to anger; but bring them up in the discipline and instruction of the Lord. (Eph. 6:4)

In his letter to the Colossians, Paul stated this truth more specifically:

> *Fathers*, do not exasperate your children, so that they will not lose heart. (3:21)

A self-centered, self-willed father can easily create intense anger and resentment in his children. This should not surprise us, because this kind of behavior creates anger and resentment in all of us. I'm amazed at how often we expect children to tolerate our adult weaknesses and immature behavior to a greater degree than we tolerate the same kind of behavior in ourselves or in other adults.

What Causes Self-Centered Behavior?

Some of us have learned to be self-centered and self-willed. We're spoiled and conceited. We were overindulged as children. We always had our own way, and we still want our own way as adults.

Unfortunately, becoming a Christian doesn't automatically turn us into unselfish and others-oriented men. In fact, we can often live a life of pious behavior in certain realms but we're selfish and self-centered in other situations. Tragically, I have seen men rationalize this kind of behavior by using biblical statements ripped out of context. For example, some pastors become authoritarian and lord it over others (see 1 Pet. 5:2–3). They use their God-ordained position inappropriately to cover up their own weaknesses and insecurities.

I have also seen husbands rationalize self-centered behavior because God says they are to function as "the head" of their wives.

Again, they use their positions of authority to become authoritarian, domineering, and controlling. Somehow they do not see that this is a total contradiction to loving their wives just as Christ loved them (see Eph. 5:25).

For several years, I conducted an open-line talk show in Dallas. People called the radio station to talk about any concerns they had. I'll never forget receiving a call from a young man whose wife had just left him.

"What happened?" I asked.

"Well," he said, "she believes that I'm too controlling—that I'm too much in charge."

"Are you?" I asked.

"I'm just trying to do what God says I should do," he responded. "Didn't God say that I was to rule over her?"

How tragic! I went on to explain that what he was doing was the *result* of sin entering the world—not a command from God!

Childhood Repression

Some people become extremely self-willed for another basic reason. It's much more complex and difficult to understand. At times the reason for this kind of self-centered behavior is hard to comprehend by the person himself. When you're talking about the problem, a person may blurt out, "I really don't know why I am so negative" or "I really don't understand my selfishness."

A Child's Self-Willed Phase

Self-willed behavior often relates to early childhood. Between ages two and three, a child goes through a God-created self-willed phase. It's normal and natural—a time when they transition from extreme dependency to independence. It's biological as well as psychological. The child begins to learn to control the world around him, including people.

A Child's Greatest Gift

Many parents misunderstand this phase. They fear that their children are becoming overly strong willed and may grow up trying to control others the rest of their lives. Rather than seeing this natural bent as one of God's greatest gifts that needs to be channeled and directed, they resist it and try to break the child's will, which can cause intense anger. If the child expresses that anger overtly, it only leads to more conflict with the parent. Consequently, to stay out of trouble, many children repress these strong, aggressive feelings. Often these emotions are buried deep within them.

Unfortunately, this approach to child rearing often produces the opposite result. Rather than developing social skills that are more acceptable—which automatically happens at about age three or four when the will is naturally channeled—the child grows into a strongly self-willed person. This kind of person—even as an adult—has difficulty understanding why he or she is so self-centered and hard to get along with. But it's relatively easy to explain when you understand the psychological roots. Unfortunately, it's not as easy to overcome the problem.

On the other hand, an overly restricted child can also become weak willed. Children simply give up, become overly cooperative and are fearful to assert themselves for the rest of their lives. In fact, girls particularly become vulnerable in a desire to please—to never say "no"—which can lead to devastating results. These individuals need a lot of encouragement to become what God intended them to be—people who properly assert themselves without being fearful of rejection.

A Child's Natural Bent

A child's natural bent is beautifully illustrated in one of the proverbs:

Train up a child in *the way he should go*, even when he is old he will not depart from it. (22:6)

Often we interpret this verse from Proverbs as a parent's responsibility to educate a child in the way that the parent thinks the child should go. More specifically, as Christians, we interpret this as training the child to go the way God wants the child to go.

This is not the full meaning of this proverb. Rather, we are to "train up a child" according to the way God has created each child. We are to consider the natural bent. We are to cooperate with the natural phases that are part of childhood development. When we do, we'll not be working *against* God but *with* God in helping the child to develop and accept spiritual truth in the natural context of life. This is indeed a profound truth, and it correlates beautifully with what we have learned about childhood development from the social sciences.

The Problem of Sin

At this point we must also address the fact that because of Adam and Eve and their rebelling against God, we all inherit a sin nature. Our propensity is to disobey God and walk out of His will.

How does this impact children? They too are born in sin. However, they are also uniquely created in God's image and have the potential to imitate godly models, namely the biblical attitudes and actions of their parents. This is why it is so important to understand the natural bent—which is a gift from God. The more we understand this God-created capacity, the more the child will respond to godly models and find it even easier to grasp the concept of sin. Rather than following the path that leads to unrighteousness, they choose the path that leads to righteousness and eventually to eternal life in Jesus Christ. In fact, if we have channeled the will properly, it is very natural and normal for a child to want to become like us in receiving the Lord Jesus Christ as personal Savior from sin.

Points of Action

This personal project is designed to help you overcome self-centered and self-willed behavior.

Differentiate Between Self-Will and a Strong Will

A strong will is not necessarily the same as self-will. Willpower is one of the greatest possessions we have. A spiritually and psychologically mature Christian, however, does not use his willpower to dominate and crush others. He is able to maintain a balance between having a strong will and yet be humble and teachable. The apostle Paul was certainly this kind of man.

Determine the Root Cause

A man who is self-willed because of overindulgence and the development of bad habits can usually isolate the problem quickly. On the other hand, a man who is self-willed because of being overly restricted or repressed in childhood frequently has difficulty understanding why he does what he does. The reason is that this kind of behavior often stems from subconscious motivations.

Take Action

If you are self-willed because you have always been allowed to get your own way, be thankful. It's relatively easy to stop acting that way. Allow Jesus Christ to control you. Study the Word of God. Find out what the Bible says about being a gracious, loving, and unselfish Christian and then start loving people. Stop using others for your own ends. Allow the Holy Spirit through the Word of God to produce His fruit in your life. Remember the words of Paul:

> But the fruit of the Spirit is love, joy, peace, patience, kindness, goodness, faithfulness, gentleness, self-control; against such things there is no law. Now those who belong to Christ Jesus have crucified

the flesh with its passions and desires. If we live by the Spirit, let us also walk by the Spirit. Let us not become boastful, challenging one another, envying one another. (Gal. 5:22–26)

On the other hand, if your problem has psychological roots that are difficult to understand, you'll probably need some professional help from a competent Christian counselor. You need someone who can help you understand *why* the problem exists and then help you set up goals to overcome the problem.

But a word of warning! It's easy for self-willed people to rationalize once they understand the reasons for their behaviors and then to continue to live irresponsible lives. They choose to go on in their sin, while at the same time blaming someone else for creating their problems.

Remember: God holds all of us responsible for our actions, no matter what the root cause of our problems. The Lord understands and sympathizes, but we must begin to act responsibly by using the resources He has given us.

Thinking and Growing Together

This section is designed for group discussion and personal application after reading and studying the contents of this chapter:

Suggestions for Discussion and Application

renewal.tv/mm10r

First, make sure someone is appointed to lead the group.

Second, spend time sharing the "greatest learning" from this chapter.

Third, use the following questions for more in-depth discussion.

- Without being specific, can you describe men you work with who are self-willed, as described in this chapter? How do these men affect you and others they associate with closely?

- Have you ever had a problem with being self-willed? How has it affected your relationship with your wife? Your children? Other fellow Christians?
- If you have ever struggled with this problem, can you describe the main cause? Would you be willing to share it with us?
- How are you overcoming this problem? What progress have you made?

Set a Goal

Write out one goal you'd like to achieve as a result of this study.

_____

_____

_____

_____

_____

_____

_____

Pray for One Another

Once each man has written out a goal, allow time to share the goals with others and to pray for each other.

Note: No one in the group should feel forced to share or pray. On the other hand, no one should be excluded from participating.

11

Handling Anger Appropriately

Not quick-tempered
Titus 1:7

"Be Angry, and Yet Do Not Sin" (Eph. 4:26)

I grew up in an environment where I came to believe that angry feelings were inappropriate—even sinful. My late father, although a wonderful, loving, and caring man, tended to be passive. I don't remember him really losing his temper, although he faced situations that would cause the average man to explode. I came to admire that quality. I later discovered, however, that Dad often repressed his negative feelings. Like so many people, he was definitely angry inwardly, and in retrospect, I now recognize his passive-aggressive behavior.

A Personal Message from Gene

renewal.tv/mm11i

As a young boy who loved his father, I naturally personalized his approach in handling my own anger. I learned to repress my feelings, just like my dad did. Consequently, I too developed some passive-aggressive tendencies.

As I began to gain insights regarding this dynamic in my life, I had to relearn how to handle anger. Though it took time, I began to stop denying that I felt these emotions, although I discovered that repression had become an almost automatic response. I also began to understand my own passive-aggressive reactions and how to express anger in a more biblical fashion.

Anger Is Normal

It's impossible to live without getting angry. It's a natural, God-created emotion. This is why Paul wrote, "Be angry, and yet do not sin" (Eph. 4:26). To deny this emotion in others and ourselves can lead to some serious psychological, spiritual, and even physical problems.

> To deny anger in others and ourselves can lead to some serious psychological, spiritual, and even physical problems.

Jesus Christ, the perfect Son of God, demonstrated that it's possible to express anger without sinning when He drove the money changers from the Temple. Seeing them exploiting others in the house of God, He overturned their tables and scattered their money all over the courtyard. He also made a whip out of cords and drove the sheep and cattle out of the temple area (see John 2:13–17). He, of course, was the Son of God; however, at the same time, He was human, expressing a very human emotion—which we all have.

When Does Anger Become Sinful?

Quick-Tempered Behavior

We all know people who consistently "fly off the handle." They're quick-tempered, allowing angry feelings to get out of control. The word Paul used in Titus 1:7 literally means passionate.

A quick-tempered person loses his cool and usually says and does things that hurt and offend others. This is anger that can very quickly become sinful—and can be very destructive.

For example, on one occasion, I was enjoying a hamburger at McDonald's. A young mother sitting at another table suddenly began to verbally and mercilessly attack her young son. He must have been about five or six years old. I don't know what he did to irritate her (maybe he spilled something), but I'll never forget his response to her angry outburst. I could see him withdraw physically and emotionally, reflecting horrible humiliation on his face. He never said a word, nor did he cry. He simply withered like a green plant sprayed with powerful poison.

This mother's verbal abuse didn't stop inside the restaurant. Minutes later they crossed the parking lot, and before getting into the car, she cut loose again. This time she came at him with a pointed finger and strong language. She must have verbally abused him for a full two minutes as the little guy turned his head away trying to escape this psychological beating.

You might guess what she screamed when he looked away. "Turn and look at me!" I clearly remember his efforts as he tried to raise his eyes and look into her ugly countenance.

By this time, I was becoming angry—so much so I wanted to intervene—though I restrained myself. Obviously, I didn't know all the factors involved, but I was sure of one thing: she was an angry, frustrated woman, and this little fellow was a scapegoat. No matter what he did, the mother's behavior reflected a quick-tempered and verbally abusive woman.

Don't misunderstand. I am not saying children do not need discipline. However, we should avoid publicly embarrassing our children. And we should never displace our own anger on them, no matter what they have done.

Verbal abuse can be more devastating than physical abuse. It inevitably creates harmful anger in children. If they try to retaliate, they get into more trouble. Consequently, to protect themselves they often repress their angry feelings. When this happens, those repressed feelings will show up in other ways—which is often passive-aggressive behavior.

> To allow misunderstandings to persist can lead to bitterness and increasingly aggressive actions.

Passive anger leads to depression, self-condemnation, and withdrawal. Active anger often causes children to displace angry feelings on other children—which normally brings more punishment. It's not surprising that in some instances these children eventually get into serious trouble with the law and even end up in prison.

Bitterness

In the same reference, Paul spoke directly to this kind of anger. When Paul exhorted the Ephesians to "be angry and yet do not sin," he followed this instruction with these words:

Do not let the sun go down on your anger, and do not give the devil an opportunity. (Eph. 4:26b–27)

Practically speaking, when we experience intense anger, we need a cooling-off period. It's virtually impossible to flip a switch and dissipate these feelings. Time becomes our friend. It gives us an opportunity to understand what has caused our anger and to become more objective. In essence, this is what Paul is saying in his letter to the Ephesians.

Personally, I have found it helpful to avoid writing letters or making telephone calls when I'm feeling intense anger. If I do write a letter when I'm feeling this way—which can be good therapy—I always try to hold the letter for at least twenty-four hours. Normally, I then make a lot of changes because I have become a lot more objective.

In most instances, I also have someone else who is close to the situation and knows the circumstances read the letter and give me feedback. On occasions, I have been advised not to send the letter at all. At that point, it's better to pick up the telephone and talk to the person directly, especially after having developed more objectivity.

Vindictive Behavior

It's natural to want to hurt those who hurt us—to get even. But that, God says, is not our right or our responsibility. Paul wrote, "Never pay back evil for evil to anyone. . . . Never take your own revenge, beloved, but leave room for the wrath of God, for it is written, 'Vengeance is Mine, I will repay,' says the Lord" (Rom. 12:17, 19). It's God's will for all of us to "not be overcome by evil, but overcome evil with good" (v. 21).

Violent Behavior

Unchecked angry feelings can lead to violence and abuse. It's the next characteristic we'll look at in Paul's list (see chapter 12). The concept means to be a "striker"—to hurt people through physical force. This is why parents should be very careful when disciplining children. If we're not careful, we'll allow anger—and we will get angry—to cause us to sin against God and our children. Out of control anger can lead to out of control physical discipline—which is definitely sinful!

What Causes Anger?

We are made in God's image.

God is both a God of love and a God of anger. Because we are made in His image, we have the capacity to experience both of these emotions.

We are born with a sin nature.

Here's a question! Did Adam and Eve experience anger before they disobeyed God and introduced sin into the world? Frankly, I'm not certain. If they did, it would not have been sinful anger.

But one thing is certain. Once sin entered the human race because of their sin, it opened the door to sinful anger! Sadly, their son, Cain, demonstrated this kind of wickedness when he "became very angry" and took his brother's life (Gen. 4:5–8).

We have been exposed to bad examples.

Angry people nurture anger in others. This is why Solomon wrote:

Do not associate with a man given to anger; or go with a hot-tempered man, or you will learn his ways, and find a snare for yourself. (Prov. 22:24–25)

This is an especially serious problem when a bad model is a child's parents. Children cannot remove themselves from a negative home environment.

Don't misunderstand. Our children need good models, not perfect models. They need to be able to watch adults demonstrate how to handle the God-created capacity to become angry in mature and appropriate ways.

Remember, too, that children can understand anger. If we totally hide our own anger from them, they may grow up thinking it is wrong to have angry feelings. This can lead to intense guilt feelings on their part when they feel anger.

I remember one incident when my son was about eight or nine years old. He was stirring his iced tea and kept clinking the spoon against the side of the glass. Frankly, it irritated me. I had a pretty rough day and just the sound of the consistent clinking got on my nerves. I asked him to stop—and he did, for a few seconds.

Once again I asked him to stop, this time with a little more intensity. Again he cooperated—for a few seconds.

The third time it happened, I turned to him, asked him to look me straight in the eyes, and said with more intensity than ever, "Kenton, I've asked you to stop two times already. Now please obey me. That noise makes me angry!"

My son looked at me somewhat startled. Then with a calm spirit, he said, "Oh, okay, Dad! I understand." This time he stopped. He heard me share my anger in a direct but nonabusive way. *That* he understood. With few exceptions, all children do!

We have developed bad habits.

Because of our sin nature, we can quickly learn to manipulate others with anger—either with outbursts or in passive-aggressive ways. We become self-centered! We have simply developed a bad habit—using anger for our own benefit.

We all experience insecurity.

All of us have elements of insecurity. It's part of being human and living in a fallen world. We are surrounded by imperfect people who discourage us rather than help us to feel secure and accepted by others.

Unfortunately, some people handle their own insecurities with hurtful anger. They strike out verbally or even physically. Sadly, this only compounds the problem since it leads to more rejection and social isolation. In worst-case scenarios, our prisons are populated with very insecure human beings.

We have been physically abused.

Sadly, physical and emotional abuse is becoming more common in our culture. Unfortunately, children are most often the victims, although more and more the battered spouse syndrome is emerging.

Most women who are victims are battered physically. Most men who are victims are battered psychologically.

For children particularly, this is one of the most difficult problems to overcome. They need understanding adults who can help them discern the source of their emotional and spiritual problems caused by this abuse. In fact, adults need the same help from understanding pastors and counselors. Unfortunately, without insight, support, and God's help, parents tend to repeat their own abuse in the lives of their children!

Points of Action

The following project is designed to help you overcome sinful anger.

Develop a Proper Biblical Perspective on Anger

Ask yourself the following questions and answer "yes" or "no." Be as honest as possible.

- ☐ Do I get angry quickly and frequently?
- ☐ Do I allow angry feelings to persist and linger?
- ☐ Do I take matters into my own hands and get even with others who make me angry?

If you answer "yes" to any of these questions, you are to one degree or another facing a personal anger problem that has become sinful. Begin by confessing this sin to God and claiming ongoing forgiveness through the blood of Christ (see 1 John 1:9).

Remember: You must be honest with God. Don't try to fake an anger problem with the Lord. Tell Him exactly how you feel. Acknowledge your sinful actions. Confess this sin and ask Him to help you overcome this problem.

Isolate the Cause or Causes of Your Anger

Other than your propensity to engage in sinful anger because of your sin nature, are you angry because:

☐ You've had bad parental models?
☐ You've developed into a self-centered person?
☐ You've had an overly restrictive childhood?
☐ You've been abused and mistreated?
☐ You battle feelings of insecurity?

Remember: Most anger problems have multiple causes. To understand these causes and to overcome the problem, you will probably need to talk with someone you can trust, someone who will listen objectively and help you isolate and understand the causes.

Take Action to Overcome Your Problem

☐ Regardless of the cause of your sinful anger, don't continue to blame your problem on someone else—even if they have caused it!
☐ Don't take revenge. Allow God to make things right.
☐ Develop understanding and insight. Meditate on the following Proverbs:

> He who is slow to anger has *great understanding*. (14:29)
> He who restrains his words has *knowledge*, and he who has a cool spirit is a man of understanding. (17:27)
> A man's *discretion* makes him slow to anger. (19:11)

These proverbs give all of us a very important principle: The more we understand the circumstances that cause anger in others and ourselves, the more we will be able to control that anger and handle it in others and ourselves.

137

☐ Learn to overcome your anger problem through an intelligent and rational approach.

Some counselors believe that people can overcome anger simply by expressing that anger in non-hurtful ways. To a certain extent, this may be helpful. More recent research reveals, however, that if this kind of behavior is encouraged on a persistent basis, it will simply reinforce bad habits. In other words, having an adult consistently react in childish ways cannot ultimately solve a childhood problem. At some point, we must approach the problem rationally and responsibly.

Personally, I try to avoid responding verbally to a person or situation when my feelings are unusually intense. If I do respond, I usually say things I regret.

Remember: It's not wrong to share our feelings of anger. But when we do, we should not attack the other person. For example, I might say, "I'm feeling very angry right now. I feel threatened, hurt, and misunderstood, though I'm sure I don't understand all the factors involved."

Normally this is always true, even though we may feel we have an accurate perspective at the moment. There are *always* circumstances we don't understand.

This approach is quite different from the person who shouts, "I'm angry. Why do *you* always pick on me? What's the beef? What's *your* problem? Why are *you* so insensitive? Can't *you* see what you're doing to me and everyone else?"

☐ Set specific goals for your life in the specific areas where you are troubled.

Preventative Maintenance

All human beings, Christians included, become angry. Furthermore, all of us need a program to keep our emotions under control. The following are some suggestions:

- Stay in tune spiritually. Avoid getting out of fellowship with God. Keep your prayer life in order and listen to the voice of God as He speaks through the Scriptures.
- Avoid having to face difficult and tense situations when you are physically and emotionally tired.
- Engage in a regular program of physical exercise, especially if you work under pressure and constant tension.
- If you become angry or upset about a particular set of circumstances and you are unable to shake the problem, learn to express your feelings in an objective and straightforward manner. Don't brood. Communicate, but avoid sending "you" messages that threaten the other person.
- Learn to back off of an aggravating situation and try to look at it objectively. Why did it happen? What problems may the other person involved be facing? Ask yourself what you can do to help become a part of the solution rather than the problem.
- Memorize James 1:19–20. If anger is a problem in your life, meditate on these verses every morning before you begin your day's activities, and then ask God to help you put this truth into practice.

> This you know, my beloved brethren. But everyone must be quick to hear, slow to speak and slow to anger; for the anger of man does not achieve the righteousness of God.

Thinking and Growing Together

This section is designed for group discussion and personal application after reading and studying the contents of this chapter:

First, make sure someone is appointed to lead the group.

Suggestions for Discussion and Application

renewal.tv/mm11r

Second, spend time sharing the "greatest learning" from this chapter.

Third, use the following questions for more in-depth discussion.

- What experiences can you share in which you have seen anger out of control? What happened?
- What have you discovered is the most constructive way to handle your own anger?
- What have you discovered about the causes of your anger?
- What do you do when you feel you have no place to go to share your angry feelings?
- Do you know someone who has an anger problem and needs help? Can you share this need for prayer without violating a confidence?

Set a Goal

Write out one goal you'd like to achieve as a result of this study.

Pray for One Another

Once each man has written out a goal, allow time to share the goals with others and to pray for each other.

Note: No one in the group should feel forced to share or pray. On the other hand, no one should be excluded from participating.

12

Avoiding Destructive Behavior

Not pugnacious

1 Timothy 3:3; Titus 1:7

Face-to-Face with Murder

One day I received a telephone call that seemed sur-real. As a pastor, I've faced a variety of tragedies—but none as shocking as this one. One of my former parishioners had been killed. While she was playing the piano over the noon hour, someone entered her home, snuck up behind her, and bludgeoned her to death.

A Personal Message from Gene

renewal.tv/mm12i

She and her husband had been small-group leaders in our church for a number of years before they moved to another city and became involved in another fellowship. In fact, her husband served as an elder in this new church.

I immediately called the husband to share my grief. During that conversation, he invited me to conduct his wife's funeral, which I did. Needless to say, it was a somber occasion.

Then came an even greater shock. The husband was accused of murdering his wife. Though he admitted in court that he had been involved in an affair during the time his wife had been killed, he denied his involvement in her death. Nevertheless, the evidence was overwhelming, and he was sentenced to life in prison. Needless to say, this is a horrible story— and one that still grips my very heart and soul!

Make no mistake about it. When sin entered the world, humanity inherited an incredible capacity toward violence. This is why the apostle Paul addressed this issue when discussing Christian maturity.

> When sin entered the world, humanity inherited an incredible capacity toward violence.

Anger Out of Control

The translators of the *New American Standard Bible* chose the word "pugnacious" to describe the Greek word *pleektees*. It's an appropriate word, but it may be vague to the average English-speaking person. Thayer defines this kind of man as a "bruiser," one who is "ready with a blow," "a pugnacious, contentious, quarrelsome person."[1]

The King James Version leaves no question about what it means to be pugnacious. A mature man of God is not to be a striker, one who physically hurts others. Pugnaciousness, then, is anger out of control—not just verbally but physically. On the anger continuum, the word can describe a man who is bullying others all the way to a man who is committing murder.

Paul used the word *pleektees* in both his letters to Timothy and Titus (see 1 Tim. 3:3; Titus 1:7). In both instances, the word follows the phrase "not addicted to wine." The connection is clear. A person who loses control of his senses because of alcohol (or any drug) also tends to lose control of his anger. How many brawls have started in bars when people have had too much to drink?

Cain and Abel

Violence in its worst form began with our first parents' eldest son. Cain resented his younger brother because God accepted Abel's offering and rejected his, probably because of Cain's sin and wrongdoing in the first place. God told Cain, "If you do well, will not your countenance be lifted up?" (Gen. 4:7).

The Lord then added a significant warning:

> And if you do not do well, *sin is crouching at the door*; and its desire is for you, but you must master it. (v. 7)

At this point it appears Cain's anger had not become sinful. His challenge from God was to do what Paul later described in his letter to the Ephesians:

> Be angry, and yet do not sin; do not let the sun go down on your anger, and do not give the devil an opportunity. (4:26–27)

Sadly, Cain didn't heed God's warning. He didn't come to grips with his jealousy and anger. He "let the sun go down" on his wrath. Whether he planned his brother's death or struck out at him in a moment of rage, we're not told. We simply read that while they were out in the field alone, "Cain rose up against Abel his brother and killed him" (Gen. 4:8). Sin was no longer "crouching at the door." It took over Cain's life!

Moses's Serious Sin

Some of God's choicest servants have allowed their anger to get out of control, leading to violent acts. Moses killed an Egyptian who was beating a Hebrew. Although Moses no doubt felt justified in what he had done—probably because of his high political position in Egypt as well as his heritage as an Israelite—it's clear that he took both the law of the land and God's Law into his own hands. Consequently, he brought down on his own head the wrath of the king of Egypt, and at the same time lost the trust of the very people he attempted to defend. As a result, he had to flee into the wilderness to escape death (see Exod. 2:11–15).

David's Horrible Crime

David's violent crime probably represents the most frightening illustration in Scripture. It demonstrates that even a man after God's heart—a man who wrote the beautiful twenty-third Psalm—can commit violence against an innocent human being. In a moment of selfish desire, he used his kingly position and power to take another man's wife into his own bedchamber.

When Bathsheba became pregnant, he tried to cover his sin with an insidious plot. He designed a scheme to have Uriah, Bathsheba's husband, killed on the front lines in battle so that it appeared to be an accidental death.

David paid some horrible consequences for these sins—consequences that plagued him until the day he died. His son Amnon raped his own sister, Tamar (see 2 Sam. 13:1–14)—another violent crime that has been around since the fall. In turn, David's son, Absalom, became angry with Amnon because he violated his sister, and after two years of bitterness, he schemed Amnon's death (see vv. 22–29).

Although David was intensely repentant for his sin (and God certainly forgave him), he never escaped the consequences. His family's story is one of the most sordid and sad sagas in all of Scripture. It's filled with horrible violence.

The Greatest Missionary Who Ever Lived

Without question, this is the apostle Paul. And what makes his story so miraculous and encouraging is God's grace in his life. You see, by his own confession, he was a violent man. He approved of the first Christian martyr's death—a godly man named Stephen (Acts 7:58). He went on to persecute more Christians. When he stood before King Agrippa years later he publicly confessed that he "locked up many of the saints in prison" and "when they were being put to death," he "cast" his "vote against them" (Acts 26:10).

But his life was dramatically changed one day on the road leading to Damascus. He was on his way to capture Christians in this Syrian city and to bring them back to Jerusalem to be incarcerated. But as he neared Damascus, he encountered the Lord Jesus Christ who spoke from heaven and said, "Saul, Saul, why are you persecuting me?" (Acts 9:4).

At that moment, Saul the persecutor and murderer was born again by the Holy Spirit. He went on to indeed become "the greatest missionary who ever lived."

Years later when he wrote to his missionary companion, Timothy, he reflected on God's grace:

> I thank Christ Jesus our Lord, who has strengthened me, because He considered me faithful, putting me into service; even though I was formerly a *blasphemer* and a *persecutor* and a *violent aggressor*. And yet I was shown mercy, because I acted ignorantly in unbelief; and the grace of our Lord was more than abundant, with the faith and love which are found in Christ Jesus. It is a trustworthy statement, deserving full acceptance, that *Christ Jesus came into the world to save sinners, among whom I am foremost of all*. Yet for this reason I found mercy, so that in me as the foremost, Jesus Christ might demonstrate His perfect patience, as an example for those who would believe in Him for eternal life. (1 Tim. 1:12–16)

Too Close for Comfort

As I reflect on the subject of this chapter, I can't help but think about Nazi Germany and the violent acts committed against millions of Jews and many, many others. You see, I am German—mostly. Though I was born in America, I grew up in a German community. Many of my closest friends have the same heritage. In fact, some of the people I grew up with were born in Germany and moved to the United States following World War II.

Ethnically, I represent some of the same people who so casually herded millions of Jews into gas chambers. When I was just a young man, other young men murdered babies and then went home to their own children, held them in their arms, rocked them, and then tucked them into bed.

Are all Germans psychopathic? Mentally sick? Insensitive and cruel? The answer, of course, is a decided no. But we, like all people, are sinners. And all of us, along with every human being alive, have the same capacity to engage in violence toward our fellow human beings and to follow the leadership of violent men—men like Hitler, Mussolini, Stalin, Saddam Hussein—and other violent leaders in our own world today. Perhaps these men were psychologically ill as well as spiritually degenerate, but why did hordes of men and women who were mentally and emotionally healthy follow them and carry out their orders? Why is this happening today?

Whether you can accept it or not, the Bible teaches that all human beings have the same potential. We have a sin nature that can lead us to do horrible things and overshadow whatever semblance of good remains in our hearts and personalities. The prophet Jeremiah said it well: "The heart is more deceitful than all else and is desperately sick; who can understand it?" (17:9).

Eichmann Is in All of Us

Relative to what happened in Nazi Germany, the late Chuck Colson recounted what he had seen on network television's *60 Minutes*:

> Introducing a recent story about Nazi Adolf Eichmann, a principal architect of the Holocaust, Wallace posed a central question at

the program's outset: "How is it possible . . . for a man to act as Eichmann acted? . . . Was he a monster? A madman? Or was he perhaps something even more terrifying: Was he normal?"

Normal? The executioner of millions of Jews normal? Most self-respecting viewers would be outraged at the very thought.

The most startling answer to Wallace's shocking question came in an interview with Yehiel Dinur, a concentration camp survivor who testified against Eichmann at Nuremburg trials. A film clip from Eichmann's 1961 trial showed Dinur walking into the courtroom, stopping short and seeing Eichmann for the first time since the Nazis had sent him to Auschwitz 18 years earlier. Dinur began to sob uncontrollably, and then fainted, collapsing in a heap on the floor as the presiding judicial officer pounded his order in the crowded courtroom.

Was Dinur overcome by hatred? Fear? Horrid memories? No, it was none of these. Rather, as Dinur explained to Wallace, all at once he realized Eichmann was not the god-like officer who had sent so many to their deaths. This Eichmann was an ordinary man. "I was afraid about myself," said Dinur, ". . . I saw that I am capable to do this. I am . . . exactly like he."

Wallace's subsequent summation of Dinur's terrible discovery— "Eichmann is in all of us"—is a horrifying statement; but it indeed captures the central truth about man's nature. For as a result of the Fall, sin is in each of us—not just the susceptibility to sin, but sin itself.[2]

When It Hits Home

The reality of what Chuck Colson pointed out in his editorial hit me one day in a personal way. My daughter had a scary experience when she was driving to work. While pulling up to a stoplight, she inadvertently and unintentionally irritated a driver in another car.

The driver jumped out of his car, ran up to hers, and tried to pull open her door. Fortunately, it was locked. He next proceeded to beat his fists against her windows, trying to smash them in. He also pounded the hood and kicked the side of the car, and finally with his bare hands demolished her side view mirror.

As my daughter looked on in horror, she noticed the man's eyes. They were ablaze with fire and hatred, reflecting violent anger. My heart almost skips a beat when I think what might have happened to my daughter had this man been able to get inside her car.

Root Causes in Our Culture

Bob Vernon, who served in the Los Angeles Police Department for thirty-seven years, points out in his book *L. A. Justice* that the problems in our society have many root causes. But in terms of violence, Vernon made the following penetrating analysis:

> Valuing material things and money above people is one of the true root causes of our culture's destruction. When the material is apprized more than people, people lose self-esteem and regard for others.
>
> Many people today lack a healthy sense of self-worth. The intensity of the problem varies from person to person, but at the extreme end of the continuum are those who hate themselves. They see no value in themselves. Their lives are miserable. And if they're just a bunch of garbage waiting to decay, so is everyone else.
>
> Those who have reached this extreme are very dangerous. They're angry and bitter. Life for them is a grievous, sour joke, something to dull with drugs and sex until it mercifully ends. Since that's their view, it's easy to end the "worthless" life of another. When self-respect is nonexistent, so is respect for others.
>
> In the inner city, the overemphasis on possessions is obvious. Many young lives have been snuffed out for a leather jacket, a ghetto blaster, or a pair of Air Jordans.[3]

Domestic Violence

The national coalition against domestic violence defines this kind of behavior as "the willful intimidation, physical assault, battery, sexual assault, and/or other abusive behavior perpetrated by an intimate partner against another." In terms of the presence of domestic violence, they conclude "it is an epidemic affecting individuals in every community, regardless of age, economic status, race, religion, nationality, or educational background. Violence against women is often accompanied by emotionally abusive and controlling behavior, and thus is part of a systematic pattern of dominance and control. Domestic violence results in physical injury, psychological trauma, and sometimes death. The consequences of domestic violence can cross generations that truly last a lifetime."[4]

Though the apostle Paul did not become this specific when he used the term "violence," he was certainly implying all kinds of domestic aggression. Furthermore, he would certainly agree that much of this kind of violence is precipitated and perpetuated by men. And so today, here are some startling statistics from our own culture:

- One in five women has experienced an attempted or completed rape.
- During one year in the United States, more than 10 million women are abused by an intimate partner.
- 19.3 million women in the United States have been stalked in their lifetime.
- 1 in 15 children are exposed to intimate partner violence each year, and 90 percent of those children are eyewitnesses.
- Intimate partner violence accounts for 15 percent of all violent crime.[5]

Our Most Violent Crime

One of the most violent tragedies that occurs every day is that an average of 180 babies are killed every hour in the United States. Legalized abortion is probably one of the greatest crimes against humanity that exists in our society. In essence, how far have we come from the crimes of Nazi Germany? How far are we from what happened in the Roman Empire? How does God view what is happening in a nation that was built on the Hebrew-Christian ethic which is embodied in the Ten Commandments—but that has virtually been discounted when making moral and ethical decisions?

Points of Action

The project designed for overcoming a quick temper in the previous chapter is also applicable to overcoming violent behavior. But here are some additional suggestions for dealing with anger:

Be Sure You Are Not Striking Out at People Verbally

Ask yourself the following questions:

- How frequently do I talk about other people's problems?
- With whom do I share this information?
- How often do I repeat negative information about a particular person?
- What kind of emotional reaction do I have when I talk about somebody else's problems?

If you talk frequently about others to a variety of people and enjoy repeating negative stories, you may be getting even with someone. This is a more culturally acceptable form of pugnacious behavior, but it is "striking out" just the same. It's sinful anger!

Make Sure You Follow a Biblical Approach to Handling Personal Offenses, Forgiveness, and Sin

Study carefully the following Scriptures:

If your brother sins, go and show him his fault in private; if he listens to you, you have won your brother. But if he does not listen to you, take one or two more with you, so that by the mouth of two or three witnesses every fact may be confirmed. If he refuses to listen to them, tell it to the church; and if he refuses to listen even to the church, let him be to you as a Gentile and a tax collector. (Matt. 18:15–17)

Brethren, even if anyone is caught in any trespass, you who are spiritual, restore such a one in a spirit of gentleness; each one looking to yourself, so that you too will not be tempted. Bear one another's burdens, and thereby fulfill the law of Christ. For if anyone thinks he is something when he is nothing, he deceives himself. (Gal. 6:1–3)

Once You Isolate Areas of Resentment in Your Own Personality, Proceed to Deal with Them

You might follow this sequence:

1. Confess your sin to God.
2. Pray for God's help in overcoming the problem.
3. Write out some specific goals to help you overcome your problem. For example, you might write, "I will not talk about Jim in a derogatory way," or "I will talk personally to Jim about the problem. If Jim hurts me, I will communicate with him face-to-face rather than get even through gossiping about him."
4. If you hurt someone's reputation, ask the person to forgive you.

Seek Professional Help if You Have a Problem with Physically Abusing Others

If you have a serious and persistent problem with anger and loss of emotional and physical control, and if you have not been able to overcome the problem through the previous suggestions, by all means seek professional help from a Christian psychiatrist or psychologist. You may need someone to help you analyze the problem and its root cause, and then support you in overcoming it.

Remember: You cannot expect someone else to solve your problem. Another person can only assist you. You must take the initiative and become a mature person in Jesus Christ, regardless of how difficult it is.

Warning: Abusive people are similar to alcoholics in that they often live in a state of denial. Until they admit their problem, they cannot be helped.

Thinking and Growing Together

This section is designed for group discussion and personal application after reading and studying the contents of this chapter:

Suggestions for Discussion and Application

renewal.tv/mm12r

First, make sure someone is appointed to lead the group.

Second, spend time sharing the "greatest learning" from this chapter.

Third, use the following questions for more in-depth discussion.

- Have you experienced verbal abuse? Would you be willing to share with us why it happened, how it affected you, and what you are doing to overcome it?

- To what extent have you observed or even experienced the kind of abuse described in this chapter? Has it been verbal or physical or both?

- Why do abused people frequently grow up and abuse others by repeating the same patterns? How can these patterns of behavior be broken?

- Why has sexual abuse become so rampant in our society?

- What can we do as Christian men to help solve this problem in our culture?

Set a Goal

Write out one goal you'd like to achieve as a result of this study.

_____

_____

_____

_____

_____

_____

Pray for One Another

Once each man has written out a goal, allow time to share the goals with others and to pray for each other.

Note: No one in the group should feel forced to share or pray. On the other hand, no one should be excluded from participating.

13

Treating Others Fairly

Gentle

1 Timothy 3:3

A Winning Coach

In looking for a man to illustrate the quality of being gentle, I was drawn to the late Tom Landry, former coach of the Dallas Cowboys. I first met Mr. Landry in his office when a friend of mine and I introduced Tom to a young man named Tony Evans. Tony was an up-and-coming young black leader—our first full-time church-planting pastor from the first Fellowship Bible Church—someone we believed could have a good influence on the team as a spiritual counselor. We wanted Tom to meet Tony.

A Personal Message from Gene

renewal.tv/mm13i

Since then, and before his homegoing, I met Coach Landry here and there—in airports, on airplanes, at banquets, and in other special meetings. I have also read most everything that has been written about his life and career.

An *Epiikees* Man

Tom Landry had a lot of special qualities. But one stands out that illustrates what Paul had in mind when he used the word *epiikees* in his letter to Timothy. He was fair minded—a special kind of gentleness.

Tony Dorsett, a premier running back who at times frustrated Landry, made the following comment as he reflected back on his years with the Cowboys: "Maybe you didn't always like his decisions, but he was fair. He would listen to all sides of an issue and then decide what was best for the team."[1]

Faith Made a Difference

As tough-minded as Landry could be, he demonstrated incredible patience and forbearance with the men on his team. In his book, *The Landry Legend*, Bob St. John summarizes Tom's approach: "His faith certainly was a factor in helping him to try to understand and cope with the much-troubled Dwayne Thomas and be more fair and understanding of a person such as Thomas (Hollywood) Henderson and the somewhat different behavior patterns of Tony Dorsett."[2]

Randy White, an all-pro defensive lineman, put it this way: "Hey, I was there when he had a lot of those misfits, and Coach Landry would bend over backwards in giving them a second and even a third chance. That's two or three more than they'd have gotten from anybody else—or from anybody in any other kind of business. He did it because he has faith in people."[3]

Mike Ditka, who both played for the Cowboys and later coached in the NFL, added, "Tom Landry is probably the fairest guy I've ever been around. He let a lot of players push him to the limit. But when they did, that was it!"[4]

Life Before Christ

Tom Landry was not always this kind of "gentle" and "fair-minded" man. His life as an NFL coach began to change dramatically when he became a Christian. On one occasion, an older fan (a man who appeared to be in his 60s) stopped Landry and made this comment: "Tom, I saw you play when you were with the Giants. You seem so calm now. But you used to get pretty mad in those days. Yes, you had a temper alright. You were awfully fiery." Landry responded, "I guess we all grow a little, mature a little."[5]

Landry's Greatest Moment

As most people who follow professional football know, Landry's brilliant career as an NFL coach came to a disappointing end when the Cowboy's new owner, Jerry Jones, fired him. Because it was horribly mishandled, which Jones has admitted, Dallas fans and coaches around the league were appalled and angry. But in many respects, this was Landry's greatest moment to be a witness for Jesus Christ—and he rose to the occasion. When other lesser men would have allowed the sun to go down on their anger, Landry faced the situation as a mature Christian should.

"I'm Not Bitter at All"

Though desperately hurt, Landry responded, "I'm not bitter at all. I knew what I was doing when I tried to bring this club back. This is the worst scenario, I guess, that could have happened. But I took that chance. . . . Things could have been handled better but you have somebody coming in who is awful new to this environment we live in. I'm sure he was very excited about the possibility of owning the Cowboys, and I doubt his thoughts went much further than that."[6]

Gentle and Considerate

I have chosen this Tom Landry illustration because it isn't often we find a Christian man who has been so well-known in a high-profile sports environment and who also demonstrated so dramatically what Paul had in mind with the word *epiikees*. Strange as it seems, it is a form of gentleness and patience that is unique. Translators of *The Amplified Bible* capture this meaning with these words: "Not combative but *gentle* and *considerate*, not quarrelsome but forbearing and peaceable" (1 Tim. 3:3). Thayer defines the word as being "equitable" and "fair."[7]

Paul's Example

When the apostle Paul wrote to Timothy, outlining characteristics of Christian maturity, he modeled these qualities in his own life, including *epiikees*.

Confronting the Corinthians

When Paul wrote to the Corinthians, many of whom were falsely accusing him, he said, "Now I, Paul, myself urge you by the *meekness* and *gentleness* of Christ" (2 Cor. 10:1). Here the word "gentleness" is the same basic word Paul used in the list of qualities in his letter to Timothy.

If you read Paul's additional comments, however, he didn't mince words with the Corinthian Christians. He pointed out their sins, defended his apostleship, and exhorted them to become mature Christians.

Paul was a gracious, sensitive, and fair-minded man, but he would not compromise Christian truth amid false accusations.

He defended himself without being defensive. People could push him only so far. In this sense, Paul demonstrated the meekness and gentleness of Jesus Christ. Our Lord, who often turned the other cheek, did not hesitate to overturn the money changers' tables and to make a whip of cords to drive the animals from the Temple court (see John 2:15–16).

A New Life in Christ

Although he was one of the most tough-minded men in all of Judaism, a man who approved of Stephen's martyrdom, Paul's life was dramatically changed when he became a Christian. As with all of us, it took him time to change behaviors that were not in harmony with Christian virtues. Yet he made those changes and became—not a perfect man—but a man who could write to the Corinthians without fear of contradiction and exhort them to be "imitators" of him, just as he was an imitator "of Christ" (1 Cor. 11:1).

Attitudes toward Unbelievers

Paul was particularly concerned that we demonstrate this kind of gentleness toward non-Christians. He made this clear in his letter to Titus:

> Remind them to be subject to rulers, to authorities, to be obedient, to be ready for every good deed, to malign no one, to be uncontentious, *gentle, showing every consideration for all men.* (3:1–2)

Overcome Evil with Good

Here again Paul used the word *epiikees.* Paul anticipated that some of the believers who lived in Crete might ask Titus *why* he insisted on treating unbelievers so graciously. Consequently, Paul explained his reasoning. First, he commented on these believers' lives before they were converted to Jesus Christ:

For we also once were foolish ourselves, disobedient, deceived, enslaved to various lusts and pleasures, spending our life in malice and envy, hateful, hating one another. (3:3)

Paul went on to remind them that although they as Christians were doing the same things, God had mercy on them:

But when the kindness of God our Savior and His love for mankind appeared, He saved us, not on the basis of deeds which we have done in righteousness, but according to His *mercy*. (vv. 4–5)

Paul was instructing Titus—and teaching us—that as Christians we of all people should show mercy toward those who are lost in sin. Although we may not be able to identify with the depths of sin into which some people fall, we must remember that it is only by God's grace that we may have been reared in a Christian home. It is only by God's grace that we may not have been trapped in the mire of sin or grown up in a drug-infested ghetto.

A Stone Face or a Gentle Heart?

Paul's exhortations describe the kind of consideration Tom Landry extended to some of the worst misfits on the team. Although they flaunted a lifestyle that contradicted everything he believed and lived, Landry wanted to see them have a chance. He revealed his heart toward these men when he once said, "The most disappointing thing is I just couldn't help them enough. I feel guilty that I couldn't get them back on the right track. Once you get on coke or crack, you're destined for trouble."[8]

On another occasion, Landry added, "If I have a weakness, it may be that I'm too compassionate. I give people a chance to see whether they can turn it around. It didn't work out for me too often."[9] This is the gentle, *epiikees* side of Landry many people never knew. They only saw him as the "stone-faced" coach calling plays from the sidelines.

Blessed Are the Gentle (Meek)

Now that we have looked specifically at the way the Scriptures describe this special kind of gentleness, let's look more broadly at other forms of gentle behavior. The following scriptural texts speak for themselves.

Prautees (Gentle, Mild, Meek, Humble)

☐ But the fruit of the Spirit is love, joy, peace, patience, kindness, goodness, faithfulness, *gentleness*, self-control; against such things there is no law (Gal. 5:22–23).

☐ Brethren, even *if a man is caught* in any trespass, you who are spiritual, restore such a one in a spirit of *gentleness*; each one looking to yourself, lest you too be tempted (6:1).

☐ *Walk in a manner worthy* of the calling with which you have been called, with all humility and *gentleness*, with patience, showing tolerance for one another in love (Eph. 4:1–2).

> We should show mercy toward people who are lost in sin.

☐ And so, as those who have been chosen of God, holy and beloved, *put on* a heart of compassion, kindness, humility, *gentleness* and patience; bearing with one another, and forgiving each other (Col. 3:12–13).

☐ But *flee from these things*, you man of God; and *pursue* righteousness, godliness, faith, love, perseverance and *gentleness* (1 Tim. 6:11).

☐ But sanctify Christ as Lord in your hearts, always being ready to *make a defense to everyone* who asks you to give an account for the hope that is in you, yet with *gentleness* and reverence (1 Pet. 3:15).

Eepios (Mild, Gentle)

☐ But we proved to be *gentle* among you, as a nursing mother tenderly cares for her own children (1 Thess. 2:7).

☐ *And the Lord's bond-servant* must not be quarrelsome, but be kind to all, able to teach, patient when wronged, with *gentleness* correcting those who are in opposition, if perhaps God may grant them repentance leading to the knowledge of the truth (2 Tim. 2:24–25).

Points of Action

The following project is designed to help you develop the quality of gentleness in all of your relationships.

Come to Know Christ Personally

Whatever form of gentleness we attempt to display, we must realize that God will help us when we put our faith in Christ for salvation, experience the new birth, and then allow the Holy Spirit to take control of our lives.

In this chapter, I have used Tom Landry to illustrate the quality of gentleness mentioned by Paul in his maturity profile. Coach Landry would have been the first to acknowledge that the changes that came into his life happened because of his conversion experience.

Though he was basically a religious man, Tom confessed to an emptiness that came into his life in spite of his great football accomplishments. He puzzled about what was lacking. During this search, he turned his thoughts toward Jesus Christ. He had certainly read about Jesus throughout his life, but who was this man, really? Landry concluded that if he accepted Jesus Christ, then he must accept what Christ said. And if he accepted what Christ said, he needed to change the way he was living his life.

Join a Bible-Study Group

Landry's search began in a Bible study after the 1958 football season. A friend had invited him to join a group of men who often met at the Melrose Hotel for breakfast, followed by a Bible study. At first Landry was skeptical. But he kept attending, and ultimately his life was changed.

He met Jesus Christ personally. Regarding his conversion to Christ, Landry made these comments:

At some period during the spring of 1959, all my so-called intellectual questions no longer seemed important, and I had a joyous feeling inside. Internally, the decision had been made. Now, while the process had been slow and gradual, once made, the decision has been the most important one in my life. It was a commitment of my life to Jesus Christ and a willingness to do what He wanted me to do as best I could by seeking His will through prayer and by reading His Word.[10]

It's true that many of the qualities outlined by Paul might be seen—at least to a certain extent—in people who do not know Jesus Christ personally. But the fact is that we cannot consistently reflect Jesus Christ and His life as we should unless we come to know Him personally. Do you know Jesus Christ in this way? If you have questions—perhaps like Tom Landry—follow his example and join a Bible study!

Pursue Gentleness

Set this kind of gentleness as a personal goal. The Christian life involves personal discipline. Once we come to know Jesus Christ personally, we not only have a new source of strength, but we also have the capacity to pursue Christian qualities. This is why the apostle Paul wrote to Timothy:

> But flee from these things, you man of God; and pursue . . . *gentleness*. (1 Tim. 6:11)

Seek Wisdom from Above

Discover God's wisdom through the Word of God and prayer, and listen to God. Remind yourself of the words of James:

> But the *wisdom from above* is first pure, then . . . *gentle*. (3:17)

Here James used the same word for gentle that Paul used in his maturity profile in his letter to Timothy. By learning God's Word, which is filled with wisdom from above, we can begin to develop and display this quality in our lives.

Converse with God

James also reminded us that we have access to this kind of wisdom through prayer. Thus he introduced his letter with these words:

> But if any of you lacks *wisdom*, let him ask of God, who gives to all men generously and without reproach, and it will be given to him. (1:5)

Evaluate Your Life

Isolate those relationships in your life where you have difficulty demonstrating this kind of gentleness. The following are some suggestions:

- If you are married, ask your wife and children to help make you aware of times when you are not fair-minded, equitable, and considerate.

- Ask a close friend to evaluate your relationships with other people and to give you feedback in any area where you do not demonstrate this quality of life.

- If you are a teacher, an employer, or anyone who supervises other people, ask them to evaluate (in writing) how they view your relationships with others in terms of being fair and objective, and if you are able to listen to all sides of an issue before making a decision.

- Develop a regular Bible-study program with at least one other man. There is no substitute for the Scriptures in serving as a mirror to reflect those areas in our lives that need special attention.

Note: Again, consider my *Life Essentials Study Bible* which includes 1,500 "Principles to Live By" with 1,500 video messages you can download on your smartphone, tablet, or computer. You can get more information on our website www.bibleprinciples.org.

Thinking and Growing Together

This section is designed for group discussion and personal application after reading and studying the contents of this chapter:

Suggestions for Discussion and Application

renewal.tv/mm13r

First, make sure someone is appointed to lead the group.

Second, spend time sharing the "greatest learning" from this chapter.

Third, use the following questions for more in-depth discussion.

- How have you developed an approach in working with people that has helped you improve in being fair-minded and gentle?

- What are some relationships in your life in which you have difficulty being fair-minded and gentle in handling people?

- How can we maintain a better balance between being accepting, tolerant, and fair, and making tough decisions gently?
- How have people taken advantage of your efforts at being tolerant, fair, and considerate? Do you feel you were too compassionate? Or would you take the same approach again?
- Can you cite the times people took advantage of Jesus Christ when He demonstrated this kind of gentleness? In what way did this happen to the apostle Paul? What about your pastor's experience?

Set a Goal

Write out one goal you'd like to achieve as a result of this study.

_____

_____

_____

_____

_____

_____

_____

Pray for One Another

Once each man has written out a goal, allow time to share the goals with others and to pray for each other.

Note: No one in the group should feel forced to share or pray. On the other hand, no one should be excluded from participating.

14

Being a Peacemaker

Peaceable [uncontentious]
1 Timothy 3:3

Mr. Charge Ahead

I have a close friend who served with me as an elder at Fellowship Bible Church North. Those who knew him best called him "Mr. Charge Ahead!" In his younger days, he was known as "Fast Eddie." He knew this trait at times got him into trouble, especially since he was a good debater—which at times was interpreted as being argumentative, insensitive, and even contentious.

A Personal Message from Gene

renewal.tv/mm14i

Before Eddie was selected to be an elder, we followed a standard procedure we have regularly used in evaluating whether a man and his wife are qualified for this level of leadership. We ask all of our other elders (and their wives) and our staff pastors (and their wives) to fill out an evaluation form on each prospective candidate and his wife (if married). This form is based on the characteristics outlined by Paul in his letters to Timothy and Titus that we are discussing in this book. We ask each person to use a seven-point scale (from 1 to 7) to express his or her degree of satisfaction or dissatisfaction with this person's behavior on all of the characteristics. For example, the first question reads, How do you evaluate this person's reputation as a Christian? (See pp. 21–22).

When Eddie's forms were returned, he was consistently marked down in several related areas, one being "contentious." His wife, however, had almost perfect scores—a threatening situation for any husband.

As senior pastor, I and one other elder sat down with this man and his wife and shared these responses. Frankly, I was nervous. This kind of communication is always difficult, especially when it is someone with whom I feel close. Eddie was a real friend.

A wonderful thing happened. Eddie sat and listened quietly. He appeared totally open and nondefensive. He thanked us for our time and candidness and assured us he would think and pray about what we had shared.

On the way home, Eddie asked his wife if she agreed with the evaluation. She did! In fact, she told him that she had tried for a long time to tell him the same thing.

The following is Eddie's account of what happened:

> When Maureen said that she agreed with the evaluation that I could be contentious, argumentative, and too bold in defending the views I held strongly, I knew that God wanted to get my attention—big time. I also knew down deep that the evaluation was correct. As I asked God for help, He made it clear to me that I needed to develop the fruit of the Spirit. He also gave me a plan. I was to get my family to hold me accountable.
>
> One evening I called my family together and asked each one to forgive me for not being gentle and to ask for their help. I explained

to them that every time they saw me using my verbal skills to steamroll over them, raise my voice, show anger, or be contentious in any way, they were to put an X on the family calendar in the kitchen. To my dismay, the next day I got five Xs.

I considered changing the rules! But I was committed and my family helped me. What started out as a crushing blow to my "Mr. Charge Ahead" ego has turned into a wonderful blessing in my life. I certainly have not arrived at my goal, but I am on my way.

The changes this man made were immediately obvious to all of us, and he eventually became an elder. How Eddie handled our communication about these issues demonstrated his desire to reflect Jesus Christ in all of his relationships. Had he responded defensively, had he walked away angry, had he left the church—as some men do—he would have verified that he had a serious problem he didn't want to face.

The Contentiousness Continuum

All of us at times fall somewhere on the contentiousness continuum, and for various reasons. In some instances, we are simply vulnerable. We may feel insecure. At other times, we are just plain obstinate. Or perhaps we've been hurt and are simply in a negative mood. We also may be getting even with someone for irritating or insulting us.

As with most of the characteristics we've looked at, Paul was concerned about the man who consistently and *habitually* demonstrated inappropriate attitudes and actions. He was also concerned about the *unpredictable* person, the man who at times is congenial and at times, seemingly without provocation, stirs up arguments and throws a wrench in the spiritual machinery that God designed to create peaceful relationships.

The Paul and Barnabas Argument

We must understand that it is not wrong to disagree or to challenge incorrect thinking or inappropriate behavior. Some of the godliest people don't see eye to eye on all issues.

Consider Paul and Barnabas. They were best friends and close missionary companions. They disagreed, however, regarding whether to take John Mark on a second mission trip. Mark had bailed out on the first journey. Consequently Paul lost confidence in him and wanted to leave him behind. But Barnabas wanted to give him another chance. Regarding this interchange, Luke recorded:

> And there occurred such a *sharp disagreement* that they separated from one another, and Barnabas took Mark with him and sailed away to Cyprus. But Paul chose Silas and left, being committed by the brethren to the grace of the Lord. (Acts 15:39–40)

This is a puzzling event. Who was right and who was wrong? Paul was such a strategic leader in God's scheme of things that it's difficult to fault him in any way. We forget, however, that he was human, and like all of us could be impatient and intolerant.

It is not wrong to disagree or to challenge incorrect thinking or inappropriate behavior.

Personally, I believe Paul was driven by a strong commitment to the task God had given him and became insensitive to Mark. Barnabas, who was known for his strong people orientation, didn't want to see this young man devastated and perhaps lost to the ministry.

I also believe Paul learned a significant lesson because of this disagreement with Barnabas, which is later reflected in his relationship with Timothy and other co-workers (see Col. 4:10). Paul became a more sensitive and gentle man without losing his strong commitment to carrying out the Great Commission in the midst of tremendous opposition and difficulties.

Barnabas no doubt learned some significant lessons as well. Perhaps he learned more about how to handle a strong personality like Paul.

Paul's Confrontation with Peter

On another occasion, Paul confronted Peter—yes, the great apostle Peter—and accused him of being a hypocrite. Paul minced no words in his letter to the Galatians:

> But when Cephas came to Antioch, I opposed him to his face, because he stood condemned. For prior to the coming of certain men from James, he used to eat with the Gentiles; but when they came, he began to withdraw and hold himself aloof, fearing the party of the circumcision. And the rest of the Jews joined him in hypocrisy, with the result that even Barnabas was carried away by their hypocrisy. (2:11–13)

It's difficult to place blame in these situations, but it appears Paul was clearly right in what he did. Peter compromised, which became a stumbling block even to Barnabas.

One thing, however, is clear. Although God greatly used the apostles to carry out His work in the world, they were human and made mistakes. They, too, were in the process of becoming mature in Jesus Christ, along with those they were nurturing.

The "Sons of Thunder"

As we've seen, the divine author of Scripture—the Holy Spirit—is open and honest. He has exposed weaknesses as well as strengths, even in God's greatest servants. James and John are another classic example. They were so contentious at times that Jesus called them the "Sons of Thunder" (Mark 3:17).

Their motives were often selfish, even as the time grew near for Jesus to be crucified. On one occasion, James and John and their mother made a power move and asked Jesus if they could sit on His right and on His left in the Kingdom (see Matt. 20:20–28; Mark 10:35–45). When the other ten men found out about it, they were indignant. James and John had stirred up a hornet's nest.

At this moment, Jesus taught all of them—and us—a powerful lesson:

> And calling them to Himself, Jesus said to them, 'You know that those who are recognized as rulers of the Gentiles lord it over them; and their great men exercise authority over them. But it is not so among you, but whoever wishes to become great among you shall be your servant; and whoever wishes to be first among you shall be slave of all. For even the Son of Man did not come to be served, but to serve, and to give His life a ransom for many. (Mark 10:42–45)

Following the coming of the Holy Spirit and the birth of the church, these men were dramatically changed. James literally gave his life for the sake of the Gospel. He was put to death by King Herod (Acts 12:1–2). John lived for decades as a dedicated apostle and in his old age wrote these powerful words:

> We know love by this, that He laid down His life for us; and we ought to lay down our lives for the brethren. (1 John 3:16)

We Are All on a Spiritual Journey

It's encouraging to know that the men Jesus chose to change the world had human weaknesses. All of them had serious character flaws, including the apostle Paul. But God changed all that—not overnight, but over a process of time. They learned to love one another as Christ had loved them (John 13:34–35).

Jesus's Prayer for Unity

No concept is more important in the Scriptures than *unity*. This was one of Jesus's greatest concerns. Knowing that the time was quickly coming for Him to complete the work He had come to do on Earth, He prayed in earnest to the Father for His disciples, and for us:

> I do not ask in behalf of these [the apostles] alone, but for those also who believe in Me through their word [all of us who are Christians]; that they may all be one; even as You, Father, are in Me, and I in You, that they also may be in Us; so that the world may believe that You sent Me. . . . I in them, and You in Me, that they may be *perfected in unity*, so that the world may know that You sent Me, and loved them, even as You have loved Me. (John 17:20–21, 23)

Unity among Christians demonstrates to the world the deity of Jesus Christ and the oneness He has with God the Father. It communicates the very essence of Christianity: "that God was in Christ reconciling the world to Himself" (2 Cor. 5:19).

God is particularly pleased when we strive to create unity within the Body of Jesus Christ. This is why, according to Jesus:

> Blessed are the *peacemakers*, for they shall be called sons of God. (Matt. 5:9)

Paul's Concern for Unity

Although Paul at times failed the Lord—just as we all do at some point in our Christian lives—he had a major concern when he wrote to various churches. Consider the following exhortations that focus on being peacemakers rather than on being contentious:

☐ *Be of the same mind toward one another*; do not be haughty in mind, but associate with the lowly.

☐ Do not be wise in your own estimation (Rom. 12:16).

☐ If possible, so far as it depends on you, be at *peace with all men* (v. 18).

☐ So then let us *pursue the things which make for peace* and the building up of one another (14:19).

☐ Now may the God who gives perseverance and encouragement grant you to *be of the same mind* with one another according to Christ Jesus; that with *one accord* you may with *one voice* glorify the God and Father of our Lord Jesus Christ (15:5–6).

☐ Therefore I, the prisoner of the Lord, implore you to walk in a manner worthy of the calling with which you have been called . . . *being diligent to preserve the unity of the Spirit in the bond of peace* (Eph. 4:1, 3).

Root Causes for Contentiousness

Our Sin Nature

When we consider the fact that we "all have sinned" (Rom. 3:23), it shouldn't surprise us that we tend to be selfish and self-centered, which always stirs up contention. Even as Christians we're tempted to reflect the "deeds of the flesh" rather than the "fruit of the Spirit" (Gal. 5:19, 22).

Bad Models

Some people grow up in this world seeing nothing but contentiousness in their family setting. They don't know there is a different way to live. Consequently, they live life reflecting what they have learned from their parents.

Bad Habits

Bad habits are closely related to bad models. It is possible, however, for people to have good parental examples but to simply grow up in a competitive society where they learn to succeed by having the last word. This is their way of winning.

Insecurity

Insecurity can drive people in one of two directions. Some become reclusive and withdrawn. They seldom open their mouths and they retreat from any kind of competition.

Others can move in the opposite direction, often becoming domineering and authoritarian. They cover up their insecurities by trying to control everyone else. Even as Christians they resort to sinful tactics to defend themselves against their fear of failure.

Bitterness

A bitter man has "let the sun go down on [his] anger" (Eph. 4:26). He has given "the devil an opportunity" in his life (v. 27).

Most often, this bitter spirit begins with feelings of anger toward one or two people and then generalizes to include almost everyone. When this happens, it's reflected in a general contentiousness— a chip-on-the-shoulder attitude that affects many, many people. (Review chapter 10 on anger.)

Rather early in my church planting experience I faced an unbelievable crisis. A man whom I trusted implicitly as a pastor fell into serious sin. In fact, his behavior was so evil he was sentenced to prison for a number of years.

During the time leading up to his sentence, he virtually destroyed the church I originally founded. I became the scapegoat for his sin—until he was arrested. Then everyone knew the truth.

Years passed and he was eventually released from prison. He had destroyed his marriage and family, but while incarcerated he had once again determined to walk in the will of God. And when he was once again a free man, he wanted to make peace with those he had betrayed—including me. Consequently, he asked the pastor in one of our church plants if he could confess publicly—and then ask my forgiveness in that same public setting.

I agreed. It was an emotional service but beautifully orchestrated by my fellow pastor. I reassured this fallen, but redeemed, man that I had forgiven him years ago—in spite of the pain he caused me, my wife, and my whole family—including the thousands of people he had betrayed.

At the end of the service, the presiding pastor gave an invitation for people who wanted prayer. In all three services, the front of the church was packed with people who were deeply moved—and no doubt had to seek forgiveness from someone themselves.

Points of Action

The following personal project is designed to help you overcome contentiousness in your personality.

Evaluate

Attempt to isolate the root problem that causes you to be contentious.

Reflect on the answers to the following questions:

- ☐ Am I contentious because of selfishness and jealous attitudes that simply reflect my sinful nature?
- ☐ Am I contentious because of bad parental models?
- ☐ Am I contentious because of bad habits?
- ☐ Am I contentious because of insecurity?
- ☐ Am I contentious because of a root of bitterness?

Be Transformed

There is no more wonderful feeling than to be at *peace with God* which happens when we are made righteous by faith (Rom. 5:1).

God sees us as perfect in Christ! This is a position that will never change. However, we can also experience the *peace of God*—which happens when we are walking in God's will—which Paul stated "is good and acceptable and perfect" (Rom. 12:2).

Furthermore, we can experience this peace through prayer—a wonderful promise outlined by Paul in his letter to the Philippians:

> Be anxious for nothing, but in everything by prayer and supplication with thanksgiving let your requests be made known to God. And the *peace of God*, which surpasses all comprehension, will guard your hearts and your minds in Christ Jesus. (Phil. 4:6–7)

Ask Forgiveness

It may be that you have hurt the entire local body of believers where you fellowship. If so, confess your sin to the body as a whole and ask for their forgiveness and prayers so that you might change your attitudes and behavior. However, public confession is not necessary unless it involves the total group. You may only need to ask forgiveness from a small group or an individual—your wife, your children, and others who may know you well.

Note: If you are confused about confession, seek advice from your spiritual leaders. They can advise you regarding to whom you should confess and from whom you should seek forgiveness.

Maintain Balance Between Divine Strength and Human Responsibility

We see this balance in all aspects of our Christian lives. Measuring up to Christ's stature and fullness is not automatic when we become Christians. Though God sees us as perfect through Christ when we become believers, we will be in process until we are ultimately transformed into Christ's image. This will happen either at death or when Jesus removes all Christians from the earth. In the meantime, here are important suggestions:

WE MUST PUT ON GOD'S ARMOR

Remember that you can only defeat Satan and be a peacemaker by relying on God's strength.

When Paul wrote to the Ephesians and exhorted them to get rid of all bitterness, rage, and anger and to be kind and compassionate to one another, forgiving each other (see 4:31–32), he culminated this letter with these words:

☐ Finally, be strong in the Lord, and in *the strength of His might*. Put on the full armor of God, so that you may be able to stand firm against the schemes of the devil (6:10–11).

Also remember Paul's words to the Philippians:

☐ I can do all things through Him [Christ] who strengthens me (4:13).

WE MUST SET GOALS

Write out *specific* goals that relate to your *specific* problems with *specific* people.

If necessary, read these goals every day. Use them as personal prayer requests. If you are a contentious element in your family, you may want to write out something like the following:

I will not start any quarrels when we are eating together. I will listen to what others are saying without automatically disagreeing with them.

WE MUST BE ACCOUNTABLE

Ask God to provide you with an accountability partner or an accountability group.

James underscored the importance of accountability when he wrote:

Therefore, confess your sins to one another, and pray for one another so that you may be healed. The effective prayer of a righteous man can accomplish much. (5:16)

In conclusion, if you cannot solve your problem with these suggestions, seek professional help. You may find it difficult to isolate and discover the root cause of your problem. If so, seek out a Christian counselor to help you understand your personality conflicts.

Thinking and Growing Together

This section is designed for group discussion and personal application after reading and studying the contents of this chapter:

Suggestions for Discussion and Application

renewal.tv/mm14r

First, make sure someone is appointed to lead the group.

Second, spend time sharing the "greatest learning" from this chapter.

Third, use the following questions for more in-depth discussion.

- Can you describe a relationship that is difficult because of contentiousness?
- Can you identify where you are on the contentiousness continuum? Would you be willing to share this with the group?
- If you become contentious, what tends to trigger this reaction?
- Do you have a specific prayer request regarding contentiousness in your life or in another person to whom you are having difficulty relating?
- Do you feel you need to ask someone or others for forgiveness? Should this be one-on-one or more public? (Seek wisdom from your study group in answering this question.)

Set a Goal

Write out one goal you'd like to achieve as a result of this study.

_____

_____

_____

_____

_____

_____

_____

Pray for One Another

Once each man has written out a goal, allow time to share the goals with others and to pray for each other.

Note: No one in the group should feel forced to share or pray. On the other hand, no one should be excluded from participating.

15

Learning Generosity

Free from the love of money
1 Timothy 3:3

A Lesson I'll Never Forget

A number of years ago, I saw an ad in the paper announcing a seminar on how to become successful in the business world. Though it was not sponsored by a Christian group, and even though I wasn't interested in leaving the ministry and becoming a businessman, I decided to attend—just to see what I could learn from someone who wasn't in my particular religious arena. Furthermore, I've always been interested in learning what I can about the business community since, as a pastor, these are the people who make up our primary audience.

A Personal Message from Gene

renewal.tv/mm15i

The speaker took a rather typical "positive thinking" approach. However, there was one point he emphasized that grabbed my attention and changed my attitude. In essence, he said that an important key to success is to always be generous—to share the benefits of your accomplishments with others. In other words, don't become materialistic and selfish.

Here I was a pastor and a Bible teacher, but what he said caused me to evaluate my own attitudes about sharing my material possessions. How generous was I?

This may seem like a strange question, particularly since my wife and I began tithing to our church (giving 10 percent of our gross income) from the time we were married. The fact is that my wife taught me to be a regular and systematic giver. She had learned this discipline from childhood. I had not. Initially I resisted the idea, particularly as I considered my salary and the few possessions we had accumulated to begin our married life. I had saved the total sum of $750 and promptly spent it on a car—an event that dates me!

But tithe we did! In our sixty-plus years of marriage we've never deviated from this as a minimum, and God has been faithful. We've not always had everything *we wanted*—but God has always met *our needs*.

What challenged me that evening as I listened to the speaker was a heart issue. Though I gave consistently and regularly to my church, how generous was I in terms of helping other people who attempted to put bread on *their* tables?

Take Tipping, for Instance

Frankly, I had always resented this American tradition. I remember when the expected amount went from 10 to 15 percent. I resisted it—until my wife gently shamed me into doing what I should. She would look at the small amount that I had left on the table and then surreptitiously she would add to the tip. Frankly,

I was embarrassed, particularly when she reminded me that she had been a waitress.

Hearing this non-Christian businessman speak, I suddenly realized that as a Christian I often gave—or should I say, met my obligations—rather grudgingly.

Guess what? I changed my attitude. I discovered in a new way that true generosity involves not only *what* we give, but also *how* we give. The apostle Paul said it best when he wrote to the Corinthians, "God loves a *cheerful* giver" (2 Cor. 9:7). Somehow I had missed this point in the broader context of life until a secularist said it!

> Being a generous tipper is also a wonderful opportunity to be a witness for Jesus Christ.

What changed? It's simple, but significant. I began to see paying the furnace repairman as an opportunity to *help him* make a living. I began to consider it a privilege to get the oil changed in my car so that I could contribute to someone else's economic welfare. And I now see tipping as an opportunity to encourage other people who are attempting to make a living. By the way, I now give 20 percent with joy!

An Opportunity to Witness

Being a generous tipper—particularly in our culture—is also a wonderful opportunity to be a witness for Jesus Christ. You see, I often study my Bible and prepare messages in restaurants. I know it sounds crazy, but when I do, I make sure I give considerably beyond the 20 percent, just to let my server know that the Bible has influenced the man who is sitting in this restaurant. And if I occupy a particular station for a couple of hours, I make sure I tip sufficiently to make up for the customers who would have occupied that space had I not been there.

In one of the restaurants I used to visit fairly regularly, I received a 10 percent senior discount. When I paid my bill, however, I added my 10 percent savings to the normal tip, allowing me to give my discount back to the server.

It's amazing how word spread among the servers. In fact, I shared this story in one of my messages on Sunday morning. After the service, a young woman approached me with tears in her eyes. "I'm a waitress in that restaurant," she said. "I'm on a different shift from when you're there. However, even the waitresses on my shift who don't know who you are talk about your generous tipping."

Needless to say, I was thrilled with the feedback. Hopefully these people will connect my Christian faith with my practice, and if they are not believers, they will come to know the Savior personally.

I'm aware of one church where the pastor had to exhort his congregation in a Sunday morning message. You see, after the service was over, a large group of his people would descend on a particular restaurant in the area. However, the word was out among the servers in that restaurant: "Here come those stingy church members." What a tragedy!

> Being a Christian and being generous should be inseparable concepts.

I now believe that in our culture if Christians can't afford to be generous tippers when they eat out, they can't afford to eat out. Imagine what servers think when they see us bow our heads in prayer before we eat and then leave without being generous. What is worse is a *selfish* Christian who leaves a Gospel tract on the table that explains the *free gift of salvation*.

Need I say more? Being a Christian and being generous *should* be inseparable concepts. How can we who have been *given* the greatest gift ever given be anything but generous? Unfortunately, being generous is not true of many who claim to have received what Paul calls an "indescribable gift!" (2 Cor. 9:15).

An Amazing Discovery

On one occasion, I met with our elders to do a study on what the Bible teaches about how we as Christians should use our material possessions. None of us realized what we were tackling. Indeed, we studied everything we could find in Scripture related to money and generosity. The study took us six months, meeting once a week for three or four hours every Thursday evening. To our surprise, we discovered that God says more about our material possessions and how we're supposed to use them than any other subject other than Himself.[1]

Shocking Statistics

We made another shocking discovery in our research! Statistics demonstrate that most Christians in America do not have God's work in their budgets. They include everything else—their houses, cars, clothing, food, and entertainment allowance—but not God Himself.

One of our elders at that time was the CEO of a large savings and loan institution. One evening during our study he commented that he had processed loans for hundreds of Christians. As he did with all applicants, he always asked for their budgets. "Gene," he said, "over the years I can count on one hand the number of Christians who have God in their budgets."

The fact is that if Christians planned their expenditures so that they never left God out of the picture—in the good times and in the rough times—God's work would never suffer. As it is, God often gets what is left over, if anything.

The Selfish Majority

Some researchers tell us that the average Christian gives only about two percent of his or her income to the Lord. We're also told that among this population are approximately 15 percent who tithe (give at least one-tenth of their income). If this statistic becomes part of the average, the majority of American Christians give next to nothing. There is only one conclusion: Most people who claim to be Christ-followers are not generous. As a whole we have become materialists, which is a direct violation of the will of God.

A Matter of Priorities

What comes first in our lives? Is it God or money? We can't serve both (see Matt. 6:24). Jesus taught us to "seek first His kingdom and His righteousness; and all *these things* [the necessities of life] will be added to you" (v. 33). Jesus simply taught that a man who loves money lays up "treasures upon earth" rather than "treasures in heaven" (vv. 19–20). Jesus also said, "Where your treasure is, there will your heart be also" (v. 21).

Christians who love money are more earthly-minded than heavenly-minded. To them, worldly possessions, activities, and benefits are far more important than eternal values. They're constantly seeking after more and more. Selfishness and pride take over. This is why the Scriptures warn us:

> Let your character be *free from the love of money*, being content with what you have; for He Himself has said, "I will never desert you, nor will I ever forsake you." (Heb. 13:5)

At this point, let me be clear. The Bible does not teach that it's wrong and sinful to make money. Money per se is not the issue. Rather it's the love of money that is a violation of the will of God! Paul made this crystal clear in his first letter to Timothy:

> For *the love of money* is a *root* of all sorts of evil, and some by longing for it have wandered away from the faith and pierced themselves with many griefs. (1 Tim. 6:10)

An Age-Old Problem

Forgetting God when earthly possessions multiply is not new. The children of Israel faced this temptation when they entered the Promised Land. Moses cautioned them ahead of time that this temptation would come. Note his words of warning in Deuteronomy:

> Then it shall come about when the LORD your God brings you into the land...to give you, great and splendid cities which you did not build, and houses full of all good things which you did not fill, and hewn cisterns which you did not dig, vineyards and olive trees which you did not plant, and you shall eat and be satisfied, *then watch yourself, that you do not forget the LORD* who brought you from the land of Egypt, out of the house of slavery. (6:10–12)

Moses added another powerful warning later in this passage when he cautioned them that they would be tempted to say in their hearts, "My power and the strength of my hand made me this wealth" (8:17). Unfortunately, this is exactly what happened.

The most tragic words in the Old Testament are recorded in the book of Judges, which describe what happened once the children of Israel entered the Promised Land. After Joshua had died, the Holy Spirit etched these words in the scriptural record—words that in many respects form an epitaph on Israel's tombstone:

> And there arose another generation after them who did not know the LORD, nor yet the work which He had done for Israel. . . . So they forsook the LORD and served Baal and the Ashtaroth. (2:10, 13)

It Has Happened Again

How could this be? The fact is, it took only one generation for degeneration to take place. But stop and think for a moment.

Do you realize that this is exactly what has happened in our own American society?

No Absolutes

When the Supreme Court of the United States changed the rules and began to make decisions based upon a set of values that contradicted the Hebrew-Christian traditions that guided our nation for our first 200 years, our lives changed dramatically. Everything became relative. We had no absolute standard by which to make judgments regarding morality, marriage, crime, rules of government, business ethics, and what is taught in our schools.

In many ways we have done the very same thing Israel did. As we looked about us and saw our prosperity, we concluded that "My power and the strength of my hand made me this wealth." The apostle Paul said it best. In the latter days, "Men will be lovers of self, lovers of money. . . . Lovers of pleasure rather than lovers of God" (2 Tim. 3:2, 4).

Cultural Spillover

Unfortunately, this new set of values has flowed over into the Christian community. If we are honest, we will admit this is true. It has impacted our views of sexuality, life, marriage, the family—and our material possessions.

Don't misunderstand. There are exceptions. But when we look, for example, at the giving patterns of Christians at large, we can only conclude one thing: We have become lovers of money. We practice what our worldly counterparts do.

What has happened shouldn't surprise us. It is a human tendency that has been verified throughout human history. We can become so wrapped up in the material side of life that we lose spiritual perspective. Money can quickly become an end in itself rather than a means to godly ends.

A Tragic Story

I had the privilege of sharing in a camp ministry for a week with a doctor who was serving as a medical missionary in Africa. During the course of the week, he related a tragic story. He shared about a man God had used to challenge him to become a medical missionary. This man was also a doctor. He, too, had planned to go to the same hospital in Africa. But he changed his mind and decided to stay in the United States. He became very successful, building a large and prosperous practice. From the world's point of view, he had everything he wanted. But something went wrong. After three unsuccessful marriages, and while still a young man, he committed suicide.

By contrast, the doctor who gave up fame and fortune (from a human perspective) treated hundreds of African patients every week and has seen many of them come to know Jesus Christ as their personal Savior.

This story does not put a premium on poverty, nor is it meant to chide Christian doctors who don't become missionaries and who earn a lot of money. But it does illustrate graphically that to *love money* and the *things money buys* does not in itself make a man happy. It can instead lead to a bitter and tragic end.

Paul issued a solemn warning in his first letter to Timothy:

> But those who want to get rich fall into temptation and a snare and many foolish and harmful desires which plunge men into ruin and destruction. For *the love of money is a root of all sorts of evil*, and some by longing for it have wandered away from the faith, and pierced themselves with many griefs. (6:9–10)

Points of Action

The following project is designed to help you evaluate your motives regarding money and material things.

Evaluate Your Priorities

Discover what is most important in your life. Make a list of those things that are priorities in your life. Try to be completely honest. Write down those things that appear first in your mind.

Establish Biblical Priorities

Refocus your priorities in the light of biblical values. To do this, ask yourself the following questions:

- ☐ Where is my heart?
- ☐ What motivates me the most?
- ☐ What am I doing with my money?
- ☐ Can I justify my expenditures in the light of eternal values?
- ☐ How much am I giving to the Lord on a regular and systematic basis?

Read carefully the following passages of Scripture to help you rearrange your priorities: Proverbs 15:27; 23:4–5; 30:7–9; Ecclesiastes 5:10; Matthew 6:19–34; 2 Corinthians 8:9; 1 Timothy 6:6–10.

Follow Biblical Principles

Be a generous Christian by following these eight biblical principles:

1. Give regularly

We should set aside a certain percentage of our income just as regularly as we are paid in order to systematically give to God's work (see 1 Corinthians 16:1–2).

2. Plan ahead

We should be joyful, willing givers by planning ahead (see 2 Corinthians 9:5).

3. **Give proportionately**

We are only being truly generous when we are proportional in our giving (see v. 6).

4. **Model generosity**

We should model generosity to others. Considering that the Macedonians gave out of poverty, should we not be a model in giving out of plenty (see 8:1–2)?

5. **Be accountable**

We need to be accountable regarding the way we use—or do not use—our income to support God's work (see v. 6; 9:3–4).

6. **Begin now**

God accepts and honors our gifts once we begin to give regularly and systematically, although we may not give as proportionately as we will once we have our economic lives in order (see 8:12).

7. **Give by faith**

We should trust God for future income and for the portion that we can give to God's work (see 9:5).

8. **Trust God**

God will meet our needs when we put Him first. He will not necessarily give us all we want, but He will take care of us (see v. 8).

Set Goals

Set *specific* goals for your life that are in harmony with biblical principles. The following are four additional biblical guidelines:

1. **Put God first**

The love of money is wrong. We must not value material things above spiritual things. To accumulate money for purely personal gain, prestige, and power is sinful.

2. **Be honest**
   To obtain money in deceitful or dishonest ways is a violation of God's laws.

3. **Help others**
   We are to use our material possessions to care for other Christians who are in need.

4. **Be industrious**
   We must never be lazy and irresponsible, living off other people. This is sinful (see 2 Thess. 3:10).

Thinking and Growing Together

This section is designed for group discussion and personal application after reading and studying the contents of this chapter:

Suggestions for Discussion and Application

renewal.tv/mm15r

First, make sure someone is appointed to lead the group.

Second, spend time sharing the "greatest learning" from this chapter.

Third, use the following questions for more in-depth discussion.

- Why do people get unusually uncomfortable when they hear messages on money?
- How can we keep our motives pure when it comes to accumulating material possessions?
- When is enough enough?
- What is your greatest temptation regarding money?
- What biblical principles of giving are you tempted to violate the most? Would you be willing to share this with us for prayer?
- What goals would you like to set for becoming a generous Christian?

Set a Goal

Write out one goal you'd like to achieve as a result of this study.

_____

_____

_____

_____

_____

_____

_____

Pray for One Another

Once each man has written out a goal, allow time to share the goals with others and to pray for each other.

Note: No one in the group should feel forced to share or pray. On the other hand, no one should be excluded from participating.

16

Fathering God's Way

Manages his own household well

1 Timothy 3:4; Titus 1:6

"God Is Our Heavenly Daddy"

My children are all adults, but I'll never forget overhearing my four- and five-year-old daughters having an animated discussion in the living room. The youngest suddenly had a burst of insight and said to the oldest, "Hey, Renee, God is our heavenly daddy." The oldest, who has always been more philosophical, wasn't quite sure how she felt about that comment and so the discussion continued. "But He is," Robyn insisted. "He's our heavenly daddy."

A Personal Message from Gene

renewal.tv/mm16i

Frankly, I was startled. It suddenly dawned on me that their image of God was their image of me. What an awesome thought! Needless to say, right there and then I made a deeper commitment to exemplify Jesus Christ in order to help my children develop a correct perspective regarding their heavenly Father.

Projection or Reality?

The father image is an important reality—biblically and psychologically. Sigmund Freud certainly saw the implications, but he drew false conclusions because he didn't believe in the God of the Bible. In fact, he was an atheist. His presuppositions were naturalistic. Consequently, he concluded that because people seem to need some kind of supernatural support system, the image of God that people have is a projection of their need for a father image. He believed that God existed only in the minds of people, which is a reflection of their insecurity. In other words, God is a mental and emotional projection of their inner needs.

Freud was incorrect regarding his view of God, but he was right in his observations that we develop certain ideas about God because of various kinds of experiences with parents—particularly fathers. After all, we tell our children God is a heavenly Father. Like my own daughters, they eventually make the connection. God, who is an eternal Spirit and invisible, gradually takes on the same characteristics in children's minds as an earthly father. If a father is kind and loving, so is God—in the child's perceptions. If the father is cold and distant—even cruel—so is God.

Emotional Scars

I remember sharing Christ with a young woman who had been sexually abused by her father. As always, this horrible experience left this young woman emotionally and spiritually scarred. Her feelings of resentment were often overwhelming.

As I shared the gospel with her, I explained how she could become a Christian by accepting the Lord Jesus Christ as her personal Savior. Willingly she took this step, so I began to pray, asking her to repeat after me. I began, "*Heavenly Father*, thank you for sending Jesus Christ to be my Savior."

She was strangely silent. I thought perhaps she had misunderstood what I was asking her to do. "Is there something wrong?" I asked. Her response jolted me. "I can't say those words!" she blurted out.

Suddenly, I understood. She couldn't use the word "father." Earlier, she had poured out her dismal story. The very word brought back horrible memories of sexual abuse that were too painful, too reminiscent of her experience as a child with her own father. Needless to say, as we prayed together, I had to avoid using the word "father."

Years later I talked with this woman at a special birthday party held in her honor. "Do you remember," I asked, "when you couldn't use the word 'father'?" She smiled and nodded her head. After a rather lengthy period of healing, she could now address God as her heavenly Father. Her mental and emotional image had changed. She understood what true fatherhood is all about. God is indeed our heavenly daddy!

Some Serious Misunderstandings

It's easy to misinterpret what Paul taught when he stated that a mature man is "one who manages his own household well, keeping his children under control with all dignity" (1 Tim. 3:4). Let's look at what Paul *does not* mean.

Paul Was Not Specifying That It Is Necessary to Be Married and Have Children to Be a Spiritual Leader in the Church

It's true that Paul outlined this characteristic of "managing his own household well" for those who were appointed to be elders and pastors in local churches. However, he was not saying a man *must* be married or have children to be qualified. If this is what he meant, he would have excluded himself as well as Timothy and Titus since they may never have married. That would be rather strange indeed since their positions in the church world were at an even higher level than the elders and pastors in local churches.

Rather, Paul was simply saying that *if* a man *is married* and *if* he *has children*, then he should have a well ordered household. It follows, of course, that if a man becomes a spiritual leader before he has children, and then eventually fails to measure up to Paul's criteria, he should evaluate whether or not he should continue as a spiritual leader in the church.

Paul Was Not Referring to Younger Children

Several words are used to describe children in the New Testament. The word Paul used in both his letters to Timothy and Titus is a general word used for offspring. This word could be used to refer to small children, but the total context indicates that Paul was referring to adult children. For example, he used the terms "dissipation" and "rebellion" (Titus 1:6). These words refer to a person who is living a riotous and immoral life, characteristics that could only be true of an older offspring.

Eli is an Old Testament illustration of what Paul was saying. Both of Eli's grown sons "did not know the LORD" (1 Sam. 2:12). They were both immoral and they "despised the offering of the LORD" (v. 17). The Lord Himself described them as "worthless men" (v. 12). Consequently, God judged both Eli and his sons. We read that the "sons brought a curse on themselves," and Eli was disciplined by the Lord because "he did not rebuke them" (3:13).

Paul Was Not Referring to Normal Patterns of Child Growth and Development

All small children as well as teenagers go through natural phases of growth and development—which often reflects struggles with authority. Unfortunately, some adults conclude that when children and youth go through these natural stages and attempt to establish their own identities, they are guilty of the kind of rebellion described by Paul in these letters. The fact is that there is no relationship between these passing phases and the negative and sinful attitudes and actions Paul described regarding New Testament extended households, which often included grown sons and daughters who were married as well as servants.

Because of this misinterpretation, some spiritual leaders come down too hard on their own children for the sake of their own reputations. They attempt to get their children to conform to certain behavioral patterns so that other Christians in the church do not criticize them as spiritual leaders.

A Higher Standard Breeds Rebellion

Children resent a higher standard for themselves simply because their parents happen to be spiritual leaders in the church. And they really resent being told they are to "be good" so that their "dad looks good." Ultimately, this kind of motivation will backfire. Sadly, as children grow into adulthood, this kind of performance standard may actually create the elements of rebellion Paul was talking about in his letters to Timothy and Titus.

Performance Standards Can Be Lethal

A pastor friend of mine overheard his son being reprimanded by another leader in the church. Admonishing this young man, he said, "I certainly would expect more from you than that, being the preacher's son."

My pastor friend, a gracious and mature Christian, took the fellow leader aside and lovingly but directly let him know he never wanted that kind of reprimand to happen again.

Please understand. My friend was not defending his son's inappropriate behavior. Rather, he was concerned that his son not think he was under some kind of performance standard just because he was the "preacher's kid."

"If my son is out of order," my pastor friend said, "come to me and I'll discipline him. But if he needs immediate discipline and I am not available, don't use my position as a weapon against him." Needless to say, this was courageous and an appropriate response.

Paul Was Not Speaking of a Man Who Has a Perfect Family

As there is no perfect church, there is no perfect family. There is no perfect husband or father, just as there is no perfect wife or mother, and there certainly is no perfect child. All of us as Christians have problems in our families. As long as we are in this world, we will be victims of imperfection. Satan will see to that.

Don't misunderstand! We should certainly strive to have a family that reflects the life of Jesus Christ in all of our relationships. Just as every Christian is in the process of becoming more and more like Jesus Christ, so every family should be in the process of growing spiritually. Consequently, having a well-ordered household should be a goal for every Christian man who is married. As with all the characteristics Paul outlined in his letters to Timothy and Titus, the quality of being a godly father applies to all of us who are Christ-followers.

> As long as we are in this world, we will be victims of imperfection. Satan will see to that.

A Goal for Every Christian Man

As Husbands

We should love our wives "just as Christ also loved the church" (Eph. 5:25). We should live with them "in an understanding way" and grant them "honor as a fellow heir of the grace of life" (1 Pet. 3:7). Peter warns us that if we don't live this way with our wives, it will affect our prayer life—individually and together.

As Fathers

We should never provoke our children to anger "but bring them up in the discipline and instruction of the Lord" (Eph. 6:4). Paul illustrated this concept with an illustration from his own ministry.

> A mark of maturity, or immaturity, in a man is the way he functions as a father in his home.

Writing to the Thessalonians, Paul reminded them that he ministered among them "as a father would his own children." He personalized his ministry by "encouraging and imploring each one," which demonstrates how Paul viewed a father's ministry to "each one of . . . his own children" (1 Thess. 2:11). Christian fathers should rear not just a family but individual children in that family. Each child has a different personality and needs individualized attention according to his or her own natural bent. This, I believe, is what Proverbs 22:6 means:

> Train up a child in the way he should go, even when he is old he will not depart from it.

Points of Action

The following project is designed to help you become a good husband and father—to have a well-ordered household.

Earn Respect

We cannot demand or force respect and love. Fathers who have their "children under control with all dignity" (1 Tim. 3:4) have created this kind of family. This does not mean they have only taught what is right and wrong, but they have demonstrated biblical values in their own consistent walk with Jesus Christ. They have not provoked their "children to anger" (Eph. 6:4). They have not exasperated their children so that they have become discouraged (see Col. 3:21).

Ask Forgiveness

I remember on one occasion my son invited his friend to come home after church. Both of them were about eight years old at the time. Dinner was almost ready, but they still had time to go out to play. I clearly instructed Kenton not to go far so they could hear when I announced that dinner was ready.

A few minutes later, I went to the door and called, but there was no answer. I walked around the house and called again and again, but still no response. Frankly, I became angry. To me, it was a flagrant act of disobedience. I had made the message clear and repeated it several times.

A BAD JUDGMENT

Right there and then I determined what I was going to do. We went ahead and began eating. About ten minutes later, Kenton and his friend walked into the house. I got up from my chair, marched my son into his own room, closed the door and proceeded to give him a good spanking. Explanations were minimal. After all, I had made my instructions clear. Furthermore, I wasn't in the mood to listen to anything he had to say during the ordeal.

As I emerged from Kenton's room, my wife sensitively took me aside and informed me I had made a bad judgment. What Kenton had tried to explain to me was that she had instructed him previously on an important lesson he needed to learn: to pay attention to his friend and to try to do the things his friend wanted to do while he was visiting in our home.

As events unfolded, his friend had wanted to go down the alley to the creek. Kenton, attempting to follow his mother's instructions, proceeded to do what his friend wanted to do. Though he may have engaged in some rationalization based on his own desires, in his own way he was trying to practice hospitality, to put his friend's desires first. I found out later that was what he was trying to explain to me, but I wouldn't listen.

I KNEW WHAT I HAD TO DO

Embarrassed and chagrined, I asked Kenton to forgive me for several things. First, I had misunderstood him because I wouldn't listen. Second, I had embarrassed him in front of his friend, which was probably more painful than the spanking. Third, I had allowed my own anger to interfere with good judgment. Had I been wise, I would have discussed the situation with my wife before I ever took action.

As you might expect, Kenton forgave me. In fact, we have discussed this situation several times since then. As we have talked, it has become clear to me that his intentions and motives were right. He had been caught between two authority figures, and his mother's instructions were far more important in his mind at that moment.

A VALUABLE LESSON

I have learned through the years that it takes effort to understand children. My wife has taught me more about this than anyone. We must listen to our children. We must not become so preoccupied with our own world and needs that we don't know what is going on in their minds. If we don't know them and understand them, we'll not make proper decisions, even in the area of discipline.

Unfortunately, we all have made mistakes. When it happens, we need to ask our children to forgive us. You'll be amazed at how they'll respond. In some instances, they may not respond as you hope, simply because their hurt is very deep. But continue loving them, and hopefully someday they'll respond positively.

Consult Your Wife

The following are some questions that will help you improve your relationship with your family:

- ☐ How can I become a better husband? What are my strengths? In what areas can I improve?
- ☐ How can I become a better father? What are my strengths? In what areas can I improve?

Consult the Scriptures

I have found two passages to be especially helpful. The first has helped me as a husband. The second focuses on being a good father.

1. Loving my wife as Christ loves me:

> Have this attitude in yourselves which was also in Christ Jesus, who, although He existed in the form of God, did not regard equality with God a thing to be grasped, but emptied Himself, taking the form of a bond-servant, and being made in the likeness of men. And being found in appearance as a man, He humbled Himself by becoming obedient to the point of death, even death on a cross. (Phil. 2:5–8)

2. Being a good father:

> You shall love the LORD your God with all your heart and with all your soul and with all your might. These words, which I am commanding you today, shall be on your heart. You shall teach them diligently to your sons [children] and shall talk of them when you sit in your house and when you walk by the way and when you lie down and when you rise up. You shall bind them as a sign on your hand and they shall be as frontals on your forehead. You shall write them on the doorposts of your house and on your gates. (Deut. 6:5–9)

Set Goals

Write out specific goals for developing a well-ordered household. Base these goals first on biblical principles, and then on actual needs that have surfaced during this study. As you set your goals, be sure to include your wife in your planning. Pray together about the needs in your household. In some instances, you also may want to include your children in helping you set these goals. This will help you draw together as a family. It's easier to be a part of something when you have been a part of the planning.

Live in the Present

When Billy Graham was beginning to wind down his incredible evangelistic ministry, I remember a comment he made in an interview. When asked what he would do differently if he could live life over, without hesitation he said he would prioritize more time with his family—particularly his children.

How true this is of many of us who have been in full-time ministry. I can identify with Billy's response. If I had my child-rearing years to do over, I would certainly do things differently. As a pastor, there were times that I was so concerned about other people's needs that I neglected those closest to me. I made wrong decisions.

Don't misunderstand. There are times when we must act immediately as pastors—for example, when there's a tragic accident or an unexpected and sudden death. Our children understand crises if we've established correct family relationships and priorities all along. Frankly as I reflect back, there were many times when I didn't establish proper priorities.

At one point in time I had a conversation with my son, Kenton. I know he at times had felt neglected, particularly in terms of my attending his high school football games. Since we have multiple services in our church—including Friday night—I missed most of those games. As I look back, my Friday night congregation would have understood my absence. In fact, it would have been a good example, and it may have been a better sermon than any one I preached! Furthermore, I had several pastors who could have taken my place.

During his college years, Kenton took time off to join a Colorado ski team—training and racing during the winter and doing his college work during the summers. Knowing Kenton's feelings of neglect about those high school years, I told him that his mom and I wanted to join him for a month in Colorado. And then I said something that caused an unexpected negative response. In essence, I said—"Kenton, I know I missed out on your games in high school and I want to make it up to you!"

"Dad," he said in response—"You can't make up for the past! What I want is for you to simply be there—now—in the present."

I was somewhat startled, but I understood. Kenton was saying that he wanted me to be with him in Colorado—not to try to make amends for past neglect—but to show him how much I loved him and wanted to be with him.

Those four weeks were great—watching him train, attending his races—and spending evenings in our condo just having fun. In fact, Kenton and I have written about this experience in the book we co-authored entitled *The Measure of a Young Man*.

Thinking and Growing Together

Suggestions for Discussion and Application

This section is designed for group discussion and personal application after reading and studying the contents of this chapter:

renewal.tv/mm16r

First, make sure someone is appointed to lead the group.

Second, spend time sharing the "greatest learning" from this chapter.

Third, use the following questions for more in-depth discussion.

- What do you believe are the most significant areas most men need to consider to be better husbands and fathers?
- What are some of the steps you have already taken to be a better husband and father?
- Can you share an experience where you failed as a husband or a father, and then through asking for forgiveness, you saw significant changes take place in your family relationships?

Set a Goal

Write out one goal you'd like to achieve as a result of this study.

_____

_____

_____

_____

_____

_____

_____

Pray for One Another

Once each man has written out a goal, allow time to share the goals with others and to pray for each other.

Note: No one in the group should feel forced to share or pray. On the other hand, no one should be excluded from participating.

17

Loving God Wholeheartedly

Loving what is good

Titus 1:8

Overcoming "the Law of Sin and of Death" (Romans 8:2)

Imagine for a moment what happens when a huge jumbo jet taxis to the end of a runway ready to take off. When loaded with passengers, cargo, and fuel, its total weight can reach 500 tons.

A Personal Message from Gene

renewal.tv/mm17i

If we have a limited perspective on natural law, we could only conclude that the *law of gravity* demonstrates that this gigantic machine will never leave the ground. But we all know there is another law that can overcome the law of gravity: the *law of aerodynamics*. When the pilot activates those great jet engines, the plane will lunge forward, move down the runway, lift off, and climb skyward. In a matter of minutes, what seemingly should never have gotten off the runway is soaring at 40,000 feet. The power generated by those jet engines boggles the mind.

Why this illustration? Adam and Eve introduced all of us to the *law of sin and of death*. We all know it well! But when God sent Jesus Christ and the Holy Spirit into this world, He activated another law that is greater than the law that keeps us earthbound. It's the *law of the Spirit of life in Christ Jesus*. This law can set us "free from the law of sin and of death" (Rom. 8:2). When we sincerely put our faith in Jesus Christ and receive His gift of eternal life, God's power is active in our lives—the same power that raised Jesus Christ from the dead and seated Him at God's "right hand" (Eph. 1:20). When this happens, "even when we were dead in our transgressions," God raised us up with Christ "and seated us with Him in the heavenly places" (2:5–6). This power that saved us is also the same power that enables us to live a godly life while still on Earth (see 3:14–21). Because of this wonderful plan, we can love *what is good* (see Titus 1:8).

"Loving What Is Good"

This quality is a powerful reflection of Jesus Christ as we continue to strive for His stature and fullness (Eph. 4:13). Because of our relationship with God through Christ, we can actually "overcome evil with good" (Rom. 12:21).

To help us understand this very positive spiritual characteristic, the apostle Paul described the opposite in his second letter to Timothy. In other words, to understand what something is, it often helps to know *what it is not*. Therefore, Paul wrote:

> But realize this, that in the last days difficult times will come. For men will be *lovers of self, lovers of money*, boastful, arrogant, revilers, disobedient to parents, ungrateful, unholy, unloving, irreconcilable, malicious gossips, without self-control, brutal, *haters of good*, treacherous, reckless, conceited, *lovers of pleasure rather than lovers of God*. (3:1–4)

Paul very crisply, and with four descriptive Greek words, described a person who does *not* "love what is good":

- *philautos* "A lover of oneself"
- *philarguros* "A lover of money"
- *philedonos* "A lover of pleasure"
- *aphilagathos* "Haters of good"

Lovers of Self

Paul was certainly not teaching that we shouldn't feel good about ourselves. It's impossible to function as mature men without self-respect and a good self-image. Without these qualities of life, we'll find it difficult to love God and others as we should.

When we don't feel good about ourselves, we may be experiencing false guilt. Of all the people in the world, a Christian should have a good self-image. We are God's children. We are heirs together with Christ. We have been redeemed and forgiven of our sins. We were created in God's image to begin with, and though that image was marred by sin, it is being restored and renewed. We have the divine spiritual resources to become more and more conformed to the image of Jesus Christ.

On the other hand, when we love ourselves as Paul described, we are reflecting the "I, me, and mine" syndrome. We are self-involved and self-oriented. Our needs are central in all that we do. We are driven by self-interest. In short, we're selfish. If these things are true in our lives as Christians, we should feel guilty. We are "lovers of self."

Lovers of Money

As I pointed out in chapter 15, anyone who has a correct perspective on what the Bible teaches knows that Paul did not condemn money per se. Neither did he condemn people who have lots of money. Rather, he warned people not to love money, "for the *love of money* is a root of all sorts of evil" (1 Tim. 6:10).

Without question, it's easy to love money. Jesus warned against this very thing, stating that it's often difficult (but not impossible) for rich people to enter the kingdom of God. They have difficulty shifting their affections away from their material possessions in order to acknowledge that they need God.

But accumulating wealth can also create problems for all of us as believers. Writing to Timothy, Paul issued a serious warning:

> But those who want to get rich fall into temptation and a snare and many foolish and harmful desires which plunge men into ruin and destruction. (v. 9)

The late Robert Horton made an insightful observation. The greatest lesson he learned from life was that people who set their minds and hearts on money are equally disappointed whether they get it or whether they don't.[1] *Note:* This does not mean Christians with lots of money will yield to this temptation. In fact, many wealthy people are a great blessing in carrying out the ministry of Jesus Christ.

It's impossible to function as mature men without self-respect and a good self-image.

Think for a moment about Barnabas. He was definitely a rich man. But when the church was born in Jerusalem, and when many believers were in physical need, he sold one of his properties "and brought the money and laid it at the apostles' feet."

Barnabas was such a generous man that the apostles changed his name from Joseph to Barnabas—which means—"Son of Encouragement" (Acts 4:36–37).

May God give us more men like Barnabas who do not yield to the temptation to "be a lover of money."

Lovers of Pleasure

Again, we must understand the positive aspects of this concept. God created our capacity for pleasure. From the beginning, God wanted Adam to enjoy life, which is one reason why He created Eve. He also created a beautiful garden so that both Adam and Eve could enjoy its fruits and vegetables, as well as its beauty.

But many of the pleasures God created to be good became evil. It began when sin entered the world. Since that time, we've often taken what God created to be *good* and for His glory and turned it into something that is wrong and sinful. What God designed for marriage, we've used illegitimately and even prostituted. What God designed for sustenance, we've abused and misused. We've made pleasure an end in itself and have used it in purely selfish ways that violate the will of God. As millions have discovered, pleasure in itself is a dead-end street. It never satisfies.

Haters of Good

Paul was definitely describing a pagan mentality in this second letter to Timothy. In essence, he prophesied that "in the last days" people will turn away from God (3:1). They will not love what is good. They will be openly hostile to Christianity and its values. They will be "haters of good" (v. 3).

It's impossible to read this passage of Scripture without focusing on our own society. Today, we live in a culture that is rapidly becoming post-Christian. Even clear-thinking people who are not Christ-followers admit that people are more and more becoming lovers of themselves, lovers of money, and "lovers of pleasure" (v. 4).

As Christians, we must face this reality. We are living in the midst of a cultural war. Biblical values for many people are no longer sacred—from Wall Street to "Main Street," from the White House to the average American's home.

Here are questions every Christian man must ask himself:

- To what extent am I allowing my life to conform to the world's attitudes and actions?
- To what extent am I focusing on myself, my material possessions, and the pleasures of this life?

Philotheos—The Key to Balance

In this same passage in 2 Timothy, Paul gave the key to balance. He contrasts those who love *themselves*, their *money*, and *pleasure* with those who are lovers of God (*philotheos*). It is this love that keeps everything in proper perspective.

Which Is the Greatest Commandment?

One day a lawyer came to Jesus, trying to trick Him, and asked Him the following question: "Teacher, which is the great commandment in the Law?" (Matt. 22:36). Jesus's answer explains what Paul had in mind when he contrasted being lovers of God with love for ourselves, our money, and our pleasure:

> And He said to him, "You shall love the Lord your God with all your heart, and with all your soul, and with all your mind." This is the great and foremost commandment. The second is like it, "You shall love your neighbor as yourself." On these two commandments depend the whole Law and the Prophets. (vv. 37–40)

Note: When Jesus said we are to love our neighbors as ourselves, He was not contradicting Paul. It's one thing to be self-centered. It's another to have a good self-image and to be responsible for meeting our own needs and at the same time reaching out to others. To be self-focused is all about us—and no one else. In fact, Paul stated this balance when he exhorted the Philippians to have the same attitude as Christ Jesus:

Do nothing from selfishness or empty conceit, but with humility of mind regard one another as more important than yourselves. *Do not merely look out for your own personal interests, but also for the interests of others.* (Phil. 2:3–4)

That Your Joy May Be Full

If we love God as we should, we will live within His will as He has revealed it in His Word. Jesus reinforced this concept when He said to the disciples:

Just as the Father has loved Me, I have also loved you; abide in My love. If you keep My commandments, you will abide in My love; just as I have kept My Father's commandments, and abide in His love. These things I have spoken to you, that My joy may be in you, and *that your joy may be made full.* (John 15:9–11)

The only way to true happiness and lasting joy and pleasure that satisfies is to live within the will of God. Then, and only then, all that God has created for us to enjoy will become really enduring.

> The only way to true happiness and lasting joy and pleasure that satisfies is to live within the will of God.

Loving What Is Good Is Loving God

The extent to which I love God and reflect that love by doing His will revealed in the Word of God is also the degree to which I love what is good. Consequently, the real questions I must face are: Do I *really* love God? How *much* do I really love God?

Points of Action

The following project is designed to help you evaluate the extent to which you love what is good.

Meditate

Read the following Scriptures and reflect on God's truth, particularly the concept of loving what is good:

- [ ] He who steals must steal no longer; but rather he must labor, *performing with his own hands what is good*, so that he may have something to share with him who has need (Eph. 4:28).
- [ ] Let no unwholesome word proceed from your mouth, *but only such a word as is good for edification* according to the need of the moment, that it may give grace to those who hear (Eph. 4:29).
- [ ] For this reason also, since the day we heard of it, we have not ceased to pray for you and to ask that you may be filled with the knowledge of His will in all spiritual wisdom and understanding, so that you will walk in a manner worthy of the Lord, to please Him in all respects, *bearing fruit in every good work* (Col. 1:9–10).
- [ ] All Scripture is inspired by God and profitable for teaching, for reproof, for correction, for training in righteousness; so that the man of God may be adequate, *equipped for every good work* (2 Tim. 3:16–17).
- [ ] But the wisdom from above is first pure, then peaceable, gentle, reasonable, *full of mercy and good fruits*, unwavering, without hypocrisy (James 3:17).

Evaluate

Read the following four questions and Scripture verses and evaluate your life to determine the degree to which you are "loving what is good."

1. Do I take advantage of opportunities to do good to *all men*—both Christians and non-Christians?

So then, while we have opportunity, *let us do good to all people*, and especially to those who are of the household of the faith. (Gal. 6:10)

Remind them to be subject to rulers, to authorities, to be obedient, *to be ready for every good deed*, to malign no one, to be peaceable, gentle, showing every consideration for all men. (Titus 3:1–2)

2. Am I using my material resources to help others in need?

Now this I say, he who sows sparingly will also reap sparingly; and he who sows bountifully will also reap bountifully. Each one must do just as he has purposed in his heart; not grudgingly or under compulsion; for God loves a cheerful giver. And God is able to make all grace abound to you, so that always having all sufficiency in everything, *you may have an abundance for every good deed*. (2 Cor. 9:6–8)

3. Do I have a good conscience about my behavior?

This command I entrust to you, Timothy, my son, in accordance with the prophecies previously made concerning you, that by them you may fight the good fight, *keeping faith and a good conscience*, which some have rejected and suffered shipwreck in regard to their faith. (1 Tim. 1:18–19)

4. Am I truly concerned about the unity of the body of Christ?

Who among you is wise and understanding? *Let him show by his good behavior his deeds* in the gentleness of wisdom. But if you have bitter jealousy and selfish ambition in your heart, do not be arrogant and so lie against the truth. This wisdom is not that which comes down from above, but is earthly, natural, demonic. For where jealousy and selfish ambition exist, there is disorder and *every evil thing*. But the wisdom from above is first pure, then peaceable, gentle, reasonable, *full of mercy and good fruits*, unwavering, without hypocrisy. (James 3:13–17)

To sum up, all of you be harmonious, sympathetic, brotherly, kindhearted, and humble in spirit; not returning evil for evil, or insult for insult, but giving a blessing instead; for you were called for the very purpose that you might inherit a blessing. . . . "He must *turn away from evil and do good*; he must seek peace and pursue it." (1 Pet. 3:8–9, 11)

Dedicate

Have you presented your *total life* to Jesus Christ without reservation? When you do, you'll be able to discover day by day God's perfect will, "which is *good and acceptable and perfect*" (Rom. 12:2).

As you read the following verses, ask yourself if you have dedicated your life fully to Jesus Christ. Note that "to present your bodies" is a specific action, but "the renewing of your mind" is an ongoing process of becoming more and more like Jesus Christ:

Therefore I urge you, brethren, by the mercies of God, to present your bodies a living and holy sacrifice, acceptable to God, which is your spiritual service of worship. And do not be conformed to this world, but be transformed *by the renewing of your mind*, so that you may prove what the will of God is, that which is *good and acceptable and perfect*. (vv. 1–2)

Trust God

When we have done our part, God will do His—but we must trust Him. Note that when Paul wrote to the Philippians, he exemplified this trust:

For I am confident of this very thing, that *He who began a good work in you* will perfect it until the day of Christ Jesus. (1:6)

Pray

When the author of Hebrews wrote his letter, he prayed the following prayer. Personalize this prayer for your own life:

> Now the God of peace, who brought up from the dead the great Shepherd of the sheep through the blood of the eternal covenant, even Jesus our Lord, equip you in *every good thing* to do His will, working in us that which is pleasing in His sight, through Jesus Christ, to whom be the glory forever and ever. Amen. (13:20–21)

Thinking and Growing Together

This section is designed for group discussion and personal application after reading and studying the contents of this chapter:

Suggestions for Discussion and Application

renewal.tv/mm17r

First, make sure someone is appointed to lead the group.

Second, spend time sharing the "greatest learning" from this chapter.

Third, use the following questions for more in-depth discussion.

- Why is it often difficult for us as Christian men to *love what is good*?
- What scriptural statements in this chapter meant the most to you and why?
- What aspects of your life would you like to change in order to be able to love God more?
- Why do we sometimes fail to realize that the degree to which we love God is the degree to which we love what is good?

Set a Goal

Write out one goal you'd like to achieve as a result of this study.

_____

_____

_____

_____

_____

_____

_____

Pray for One Another

Once each man has written out a goal, allow time to share the goals with others and to pray for each other.

Note: No one in the group should feel forced to share or pray. On the other hand, no one should be excluded from participating.

18

Being Just and Upright

Just

Titus 1:8

I Almost Blew It!

On one occasion, a former student of mine stopped by my office unannounced. It was one of those hectic days. I had been up since 3:30 a.m. working on a writing project. When he arrived, I was just completing a rather heavy meeting in the middle of the afternoon and was about to crash and call it quits for the day. Frankly, I didn't feel like *seeing* anyone, let alone *talking* to someone. But I knew in my heart I couldn't say no.

A Personal Message from Gene

renewal.tv/mm18i

Although I hadn't seen this man for years, I recognized his name and invited him into my office, hoping it would only take a few minutes. But God had other plans. After some small talk, he began to unfold a sad story, one he said he had not intended to tell. After graduation from the school where I taught, he married a girl who was also one of my students. He became a pastor.

A Marital Disaster

From the beginning, his marriage was in trouble. Every story always has two sides, but I believe I heard enough and knew enough to conclude that his report was believable. According to him, his wife was always hurting other people's feelings in his congregation, creating divisions, gossiping, and keeping his own family in a state of confusion. His life as a pastor was filled with embarrassment and heartache. After a number of years, he became so frustrated that he gave up. In anger and resentment, he divorced her and left the ministry.

A Root of Bitterness

When he arrived in my office that day, he had been wandering in the wilderness for nearly three years. He admitted that he had sinned during that time, becoming involved sexually with another woman. In recent months, he had broken off the relationship because he knew it was wrong. He felt helpless, frustrated, and rejected by even his closest friends. The people in his former church had not reached out to him. Though in some respects that was understandable, he was desperately hurt and bitter.

One day he had stopped to see another pastor he knew well. The pastor was just concluding a counseling session and his secretary called him on the intercom telling him who was waiting. The pastor responded by saying he was too busy—too busy to step out of his office and say hello.

As this man related his story, he suddenly broke down and wept. He didn't justify himself. He acknowledged his anger and his bitterness. He confessed his guilt about the fact that he had finally given up and divorced his wife and left the ministry, even though four well-known pastors had advised him that he probably didn't have any choice in the matter. "But, Gene," he said through tears, "the man wouldn't even say hello to me!"

My own heart skipped a beat. I had almost done the same thing that afternoon. Thank God, the Holy Spirit didn't let me do it. As tired as I was, I sat and listened to his story for more than two hours. I literally felt his pain.

After listening, I suggested some biblical steps for getting his life back in order and in harmony with the will of God. I'll never forget his response. He looked down and tried to fight the tears. "Gene, what you just said means more to me than anything I've heard for the last three years. Though I may never bother you again and though I may not take your advice totally, I know you care, and right now I just need a friend who will listen."

I would be dishonest if I told you it was easy at that moment to be *just* and *upright* and *caring*. It's impossible for me to talk with everyone who wants to share a burden. If I tried, I would probably end up in desperate straits myself. But I thank God I didn't let that one pass me by. And the good news is, the man eventually responded and is now once again walking with the Lord.

Two Basic Meanings

New Testament writers used the word "just" (*dikaios*) in two basic ways. First, to become "just" describes what happens *when we are saved*. Second, to be "just" describes the way we should live *after we are saved*. Obviously, Paul had the second meaning in mind when he used *dikaios* to describe a quality of Christian maturity.

More specifically, when Paul used the word "just" in the list of qualifications in his letter to Titus, he was referring to a person who does what is right or fair. In this sense, a *just* man is equitable and impartial. For example, when he makes decisions, they are decisions that are "just." Stating it another way, a *just* man is someone who is *righteous* and *upright* in all of his relationships.

Thankfully, I believe the Lord enabled me to demonstrate this quality with my former student, although I almost made a tragic mistake. Often, being "just" involves making the right decision at the right moment.

Justification by Faith

In November 1515, an Augustinian monk named Martin Luther began to teach the book of Romans to his students at the University of Wittenberg. As professor of sacred theology, he labored long and hard in preparing his lectures. He was captivated and challenged by what Paul stated about justification by faith. "I greatly longed to understand Paul's Epistle to the Romans," he later wrote, "and nothing stood in the way but that one expression, 'the righteousness of God,' because I took it to mean that righteousness whereby God is righteous and deals righteously in punishing the unrighteous."[1]

A Born Again Experience

After Luther wrestled with this concept for a lengthy period of time, the Holy Spirit eventually penetrated Luther's heart. He suddenly "grasped the truth that the righteousness of God is that righteousness whereby, through grace and sheer mercy, He justifies us by faith. Thereupon," Luther testified, "I felt myself to be reborn and have gone through open doors into paradise. The whole of Scripture took on a new meaning, and whereas before 'the righteousness of God' had filled me with hate, now it became to me an inexpressibly sweet and greater love. This passage of Paul became to me a gateway to heaven."[2]

Luther's experience describes the most foundational way *dikaios* and related words are used by New Testament writers to describe what happens to a person who comes to know Jesus Christ as their personal Lord and Savior. Paul stated this clearly in his letter to the Romans, although it took Luther a long time to grasp this wonderful truth:

> For I am not ashamed of the gospel of Christ: for it is the power of God unto salvation to every one that believeth; to the Jew first, and also to the Greek. For therein is the righteousness [*dikaiosune*] of God revealed from faith to faith: as it is written, the *just* [*dikaios*] shall live by faith. (Rom. 1:16–17 KJV; see Gal. 3:11; Heb. 10:38)

Positional Righteousness

In Romans 1:16–17, and in many other references, Paul was referring to what theologians call "positional righteousness." When we put our faith in Jesus Christ for salvation, God sees us as being as righteous as Christ Himself. In fact, this is the only way any person can ever be saved. In terms of our redemption, Jesus Christ Himself is our righteousness (see 1 Cor. 1:30). This is the great truth that changed Martin Luther's life. In the words of Jesus, he was "born again" (John 3:3). This great truth in Paul's letter to the Romans changed Luther's life, and God used him to help change the world. "The just shall live by faith" became his clarion call.

This should not surprise us, because Paul used some form of the word *dikaios* more than twenty times in the first five chapters of Romans to refer to the fact that we are made *righteous* or *just* in God's sight by faith in Jesus Christ.

Justified Men Should Become Men Who Live Just Lives

Once we truly understand and experience God's grace in justifying us and making us *just* or *righteous* in God's sight, it becomes a foundational experience in enabling and challenging us to become *just* in our walk with God and in our relationships with others.

A just man is someone who is righteous and upright in all of his relationships.

It should become a mark of Christian maturity, which is what Paul referred to in his letter to Titus. Of all people, justified men should become men who live *just* lives.

God dealt with us "justly," not because we deserved it, but because of His love, mercy, and grace. This should motivate every Christian, first to live a *just* and *righteous* life before God and second, to deal *justly* with others.

Further on in his letter to Titus, Paul encouraged all Christians to demonstrate compassion, sensitivity, and concern toward both Christians and non-Christians. Paul made this appeal based on what Jesus Christ has done for us. After Paul stated that we should show *"every consideration for all men"* (Titus 3:2), he said:

> For we also once were foolish ourselves, disobedient, deceived, enslaved to various lusts and pleasures, spending our life in malice and envy, hateful, hating one another. But when the kindness of God our Savior and His love for mankind appeared, He saved us, not on the basis of deeds which we have done in righteousness, but according to His mercy, by the washing of regeneration and renewing by the Holy Spirit, whom He poured out upon us richly through Jesus Christ our Savior, so that being justified by His grace we would be made heirs according to the hope of eternal life. (vv. 3–7)

Justice and Fairness

God gives us opportunities every day to practice justice and to be upright in our dealings with fellow human beings. This involves our relationships with our immediate families, with our fellow Christians, and with non-Christians who regularly cross our paths.

When Paul wrote to the Colossians and exhorted "masters" to grant to their slaves "*justice* and *fairness*, knowing that you too have a Master in heaven" (4:1), he illustrated what he had in mind when he told Titus that spiritually mature people are "just" (1:8). The translators of *The Amplified Bible* captured this meaning when they rendered this concept as being "upright and fair-minded" (1:8).

Inexcusable, but It Happens

Through the years, I have seen people desperately hurt because of self-centered, insensitive, and hard-hearted Christians. One of the saddest comments I have ever heard from both believers and unbelievers is that they would rather do business with non-Christians than with Christians, because Christians, they say, are more unfair, irresponsible, and, in some cases, more ruthless than non-Christians.

I realize, as most people do, that one bad experience with a Christian can cause someone to generalize about every Christian. I have met believers who have written off Christianity—or at least going to church—because they have had one bad experience with a so-called Christian leader. How unfortunate. I have also met Christians who have written off a whole seminary because they have had a bad experience with a single graduate.

Unfortunately, many of us are tempted to generalize, to judge groups by single encounters. This in itself reflects injustice, prejudice, and unfair judgments. In a sense, the pot is calling the kettle black. It reflects our own immaturity when it comes to practicing the quality of being just.

A Shining Example

When it comes to being *just* in the way Paul used this word in his letter to Titus, Joseph, Mary's husband, stands out. You know the story. He was engaged to be married to Mary, but before they became husband and wife, she became pregnant through the power of the Holy Spirit (see Matt. 1:18). Needless to say, Joseph found himself in an embarrassing predicament. He was engaged—not legally married—and his wife-to-be was with child.

Tongues were wagging. But note how Joseph responded, "And Joseph her husband, being a righteous [*dikaios*] man [a just man], and not wanting to disgrace her, planned to send her away secretly" (v. 19).

If we look casually at Joseph's response, we might conclude he was simply embarrassed and trying to protect himself. Not so! He was concerned for Mary because he was a *just* man. He understood her plight and the price she was paying to be the mother of the Son of God. He didn't want to expose her to public disgrace.

God Honors Justice

Mercifully, God stepped in and reassured Joseph that their predicament and humiliation were only temporary (see vv. 20–21). The pain they would have to bear, caused by those who were critical because of their ignorance, insensitivity, and unbelief, would be rewarded when the angels sang from heaven, "Glory to God in the highest, and on earth peace among men with whom He is pleased" (Luke 2:14). And when the wise men from the East would later bring gifts, lay them at the feet of Jesus, and recognize Him as a King, it would be worth it all.

> May God give us more upright men who are willing to put their own egos behind them and be concerned for others.

Injustice Today

How many men do you know who have gotten women pregnant out of wedlock and then left them to bear the burden that resulted from a moment of lust and self-indulgence? Or, worse yet, they escaped their responsibilities with payoffs and helped the women get abortions.

Don't misunderstand. I am not putting all the blame on men. This kind of sin is usually a two-way street. But how easy it is to take advantage of someone else and then allow that person to struggle through the problem all alone. That is the ultimate in *unjust* behavior.

Points of Action

The following project will help you develop the quality of being just in your relationships with others.

A Gift of God

Make sure you clearly understand Paul's statement that the "just shall live by faith" (Rom. 1:17, KJV). Remember that the Word of God uses the term "just" in two ways. The first involves your salvation experience. The second involves the way you live as a Christian.

Paul described both concepts in two wonderful verses in his letter to the Ephesians:

1. Your salvation experience

> For by grace you have been *saved through faith*; and that not of yourselves, it is the gift of God; not as a result of works, so that no one may boast. (2:8–9)

2. Your walk with Christ

> For we are His *workmanship*, created in Christ Jesus *for good works*, which God prepared beforehand so that we would walk in them. (v. 10)

What Paul described in this paragraph contains one of the most critical distinctions in Christian theology. As we have seen illustrated in Martin Luther's life, it's perhaps the one area that Satan uses most frequently to confuse people, in spite of the fact that it is one of the clearest teachings in Scripture. Unfortunately, this doctrinal error runs through every major religion in the world, including the offshoots of Christianity that we call cults and "isms."

Following are several ways this error is reflected. Check yourself. How well do you understand the salvation experience?

☐ A person can be saved by works.

☐ A person can be saved by a mixture of faith and works.

☐ A person can be saved by faith and keep himself saved by works.

☐ A person can be saved even though he doesn't demonstrate any works.

☐ All of the above are incorrect.

God's Workmanship

Some people believe that a simple profession of faith always results in salvation. One thing is clear from Scripture: we *are* saved by faith, but *true and authentic faith* will eventually produce works. James made this point clear when he said, "Even so faith, if it has no works, is dead, being by itself" (2:17).

Saving faith will eventually produce the works of righteousness God planned for our lives. The extent to which we do these works, however, still depends on our commitment to Jesus Christ and our desire to do His will.

When James used Elijah to illustrate the power of prayer, he used the word *dikaios* to refer to a Christian who lives a godly life. This is why he exhorted:

Therefore, confess your sins to one another, and pray for one another so that you may be healed. The effective prayer of a *righteous* [just] man can accomplish much. (5:16)

When New Testament writers used the word "just" in this sense, they meant that we are to live upright, righteous, and holy lives as Christians. We are to obey God and keep His commandments. Once we are made righteous (just) by faith in Christ, then we are to reflect Christ's righteous (just) life by the way we live. This is also what Paul meant when he wrote to the Ephesians:

For you were formerly darkness, but now you are Light in the Lord; walk as children of Light (for the fruit of the Light consists in all goodness and *righteousness* [*dikaiosune*] and truth), trying to learn what is pleasing to the Lord. (5:8–10)

Your Relationships

Ask someone you trust to help you evaluate your relationships with others regarding the extent you are just, fair, impartial, and equitable.

- Your relationship with your wife
- Your relationship with your children
- Your relationship with your neighbors
- Your relationship with your fellow employees
- Your relationship with others in your life

Thinking and Growing Together

This section is designed for group discussion and personal application after reading and studying the contents of this chapter:

Suggestions for Discussion and Application

renewal.tv/mm18r

First, make sure someone is appointed to lead the group.

Second, spend time sharing the "greatest learning" from this chapter.

Third, use the following questions for more in-depth discussion.

- When did you understand what it means to be justified by faith? Would you share your salvation experience?
- Why is it easy to get confused regarding how a person is saved?
- What experiences have you had (or observed) where people have been treated unjustly? How could things have been handled differently?
- Can you think of relationships where you would like to be treated more fairly and equitably? Would you share these concerns for prayer?
- Can you think of relationships where you would like to be more just and fair in your dealings with others? Would you share these concerns for prayer?

Set a Goal

Write out one goal you'd like to achieve as a result of this study.

2222

Pray for One Another

Once each man has written out a goal, allow time to share the goals with others and to pray for each other.

Note: No one in the group should feel forced to share or pray. On the other hand, no one should be excluded from participating.

19

Living a Holy Life

Devout [holy]

Titus 1:8

Bleeding Knees

Several years ago, my wife and I visited a Central American country. In one small village, one of the missionaries drew our attention to a church that had a long series of steps leading up to a large courtyard. We then noticed people on their hands and knees, making their way up the concrete steps and then through the courtyard and then into the church. Their knees would eventually bleed as they crawled the hundreds of yards over the rough concrete surface.

A Personal Message from Gene

renewal.tv/mm19i

What would cause people to engage in this kind of religious ritual? They actually believed that this was a way they could become *holy* and experience forgiveness for their sins. Although these people were obviously sincere, they were terribly misled. Paul *did* say he wanted "men in every place to pray, *lifting up holy hands*" (1 Tim. 2:8), but nowhere does God say Christians are to have "bleeding knees" to obtain and maintain holiness.

This story illustrates a serious misperception regarding holiness. We can never earn it by engaging in religious rituals. Neither can we develop holiness by abusing our bodies.

False Views Regarding Holiness

Let's take a look at some of the other serious misunderstandings regarding what it means to live a holy life.

Perfectionism

When Paul stated that being *devout* or *holy* is a mark of Christian maturity, he was not teaching that Christians can become perfect in this life. Most of us, if we're honest, will acknowledge that we're not living in every way like Jesus Christ. He was the only perfect man who ever lived. He came to Earth as the God-man, and because He was God in the flesh, He never sinned (see John 1:1, 14).

As Christians, we'll not be totally like Jesus Christ until we are transformed into His image when He comes again (see 1 Cor. 15:51–53). This, I believe, is what Paul had in mind when he wrote to the Corinthians:

> For now we see in a mirror dimly, but then *face to face*; now I know in part, but then I will *know fully* just as I also have been fully known. (13:12)

Christians who are taught that they can become perfect in this life often suffer horrible guilt when they fail. Or to handle this guilt, they may rationalize sinful attitudes and actions as being unsinful, which is a form of self-deception and is sin in itself.

Others who take a perfectionistic approach to the Christian life simply give up when they sin. They believe they have failed God and have no real hope. Some also believe they have committed the unpardonable sin, which is a tragic point of view.

I had a close friend in high school who became a Christian approximately the same time I did. Both of us were sincere people but theologically confused in certain areas. I thought I had to live a certain way to keep myself saved. My friend believed that all Christians can have an experience with God that enables them to reach a level of holiness that keeps them from sinning.

Eventually, I learned that my standing before God—my eternal salvation—was not dependent upon my good works as a Christian. What a relief! But sadly, my friend experienced moral failure. I remember talking with her one day only to discover that she believed God had given up on her because of her sin. Nothing I could say seemed to help her understand that God had not forsaken her. Sadly, she didn't believe God would forgive her. Even the story of the prodigal son couldn't reach her. What she had been taught about holiness left her in a state of hopelessness. How tragic!

Asceticism

During the fourth century particularly, hundreds of people sought to escape temptation by punishing their bodies and by living as hermits. This happened primarily because many of the Greek philosophers taught that the body is evil and the spirit is good. Because our bodies *do* give us a lot of problems that lead us into sinful actions, it was relatively easy for Christ-followers living at that time to synchronize this thinking with biblical theology.

Unfortunately, various forms of asceticism have caused Christians to try to remove themselves from the world. This is a direct contradiction to what Jesus taught. We are to be "the light of the world" (Matt. 5:14). We are to let our "light shine before men" (v. 16) so that they may see our good works and glorify our Father who is in heaven. Paul also stated that we are to be in the world, but not part of the world (see 1 Cor. 5:9–10). In other words, it is possible to live in this world and still live a holy life. That is one of the reasons God has left us on Earth: to communicate His holiness to those who do not know Him personally.

Self-Denial

Paul was not teaching that Christians can become holy by denying themselves what God has created to be normal and natural. This too is a form of asceticism. For example, some people today still take vows of chastity, giving up the right to be married. They believe this will make them more holy in God's sight.

The Scriptures clearly teach that abstaining from legitimate sexual relations is not a sign of or a means to holiness. It's true that Paul promoted singleness as a special gift from God, but vows of chastity as a means to more holiness has led to some of the worst forms of sexual immorality in both heterosexual and homosexual relationships. Even more devastating, a false view of marriage has led to a groundswell of child abuse. Sadly, innocent people—children particularly—become victims of this false teaching.

> It is possible to live in this world and still live a holy life.

Legalism

Some Christians believe they can become holy by following a set of rules. I grew up in this kind of religious community. There were a lot of external requirements that set them off as a distinct group of people. Yet I noticed, even as a young Christian, that some of these people often reflected jealousy and pride. They were judgmental and prejudiced against people who were not a part of our particular religious community. They also gossiped about one another. In essence, they overlooked those *internal qualities* that are so important to true holiness.

This is exactly what the Pharisees did on many occasions. They set up legalistic rules and then planned ways to circumvent those rules. Jesus condemned this kind of behavior (see Mark 7:9–13).

A Biblical Perspective

Positional Holiness

All people who have seriously put their faith in Jesus Christ for salvation are perfectly holy in God's sight the moment they truly believe. For example, the Corinthian Christians, as sinful and carnal as they were initially as new Christians, were called "saints," or "those who have been sanctified in Christ Jesus" (1 Cor. 1:2). Literally, Paul called these people "holy ones" in spite of their sinful lifestyles. This positional perfection was based on how God the Father viewed them because of their faith in the death and resurrection of Jesus Christ. But because of their previous lifestyles as Godless pagans, it took time for them to live holy lives on a consistent basis.

Paul also underscored this truth in his letter to the Colossians when he identified these believers "as those who have been chosen of God, *holy* and beloved" (3:12). God, therefore, sees us as already perfect because of His perfect Son, Jesus Christ. If this were not true, no one could be saved. Theologians often call this great doctrinal truth "positional sanctification." In the mind of God, we are already set apart as His holy people. In His sight, we are already "glorified" (Rom. 8:30). This happens the moment we put our faith in Christ and are saved.

Progressive Holiness

Becoming holy and Christ-like while on Earth is a process that should continue until we are with Jesus Christ in heaven. This is the great emphasis in the New Testament letters. Again and again we're instructed to become like Christ in His holiness—to measure up to the stature and fullness of Christ (Eph. 4:13). When writing to the Corinthians, Paul addressed their sins and urged them to pursue holy lives that reflected Christ's love and the fruit of the Holy Spirit (see 1 Cor. 13).

Commitment

Becoming holy as God intended involves an act of the will following our conversion to Jesus Christ. For example, in the first three chapters of Ephesians, Paul outlined *our position in Christ*. In the last three chapters, he instructed us to *become like Christ*—"to walk in a manner worthy of the calling with which you have been called" (4:1).

We see the same pattern in the letter to the Romans. The first eleven chapters outline in great detail God's mercy in saving us. The remaining chapters describe how we are to live a holy life in view of God's mercies (see Rom. 12:1–2).

The Holy Spirit

The degree to which we live holy lives depends upon the extent to which we keep in step with the Holy Spirit and His plan for our lives. Writing to the Galatians, Paul made this point very specific:

> But I say, *walk by the Spirit*, and you will not carry out the desire of the flesh. (5:16)

Every Christian has a choice. Either we "walk by the Spirit" (v. 25) and do what *He* desires, or we keep in step with the sinful nature and do what *we* desire. Either we choose to present the members of our bodies "to sin as *instruments of unrighteousness*," or we choose to present ourselves "to God as those alive from the dead," and then yield our bodies "as *instruments of righteousness* to God" (Rom. 6:13). When we choose to yield to God, we choose to "walk by the Spirit" and to draw upon His strength and power in order to live holy and righteous lives (see Eph. 3:16–19).

> **The degree to which we live holy lives depends upon the extent to which we keep in step with the Holy Spirit and His plan for our lives.**

The Flesh vs. the Spirit

A Christian who walks by the Spirit will reflect "the fruit of the Spirit" (Gal. 5:22) rather than "the deeds of the flesh" (v. 19). Paul outlined this "fruit"—a true reflection of holiness—and contrasted it with "the deeds of the flesh":

- The deeds of the flesh

  Now the deeds of the flesh are evident, which are: immorality, impurity, sensuality, idolatry, sorcery, enmities, strife, jealousy, outbursts of anger, disputes, dissensions, factions, envying, drunkenness, carousing, and things like these. (vv. 19–21)

- The fruit of the Spirit

  But the fruit of the Spirit is love, joy, peace, patience, kindness, goodness, faithfulness, gentleness, self-control. (vv. 22–23)

When we "walk in a manner worthy of the calling with which [we] have been called" (Eph. 4:1), we will reflect the fruit of the Spirit in all of our relationships.

The Spirit and the Word

The primary resource that enables us to walk in the Spirit is the Holy Spirit Himself working through the Word of God. Writing to the Colossians, Paul said:

> Let the *word of Christ* richly dwell within you, with all wisdom teaching and admonishing one another with psalms and hymns and spiritual songs, singing with thankfulness in your hearts to God. (3:16)

Because the Holy Spirit is the divine author of Scripture, and because He indwells every believer, He enables us to live out these truths in our lives, if we yield our lives to Him (see Eph. 3:20–21).

Renewed Minds

The process of becoming holy is uniquely linked with how we use our minds. This is why Paul concluded his letter to the Philippians by saying:

> Finally, brethren, whatever is true, whatever is honorable, whatever is right, whatever is pure, whatever is lovely, whatever is of good repute, if there is any excellence and if anything worthy of praise, *dwell on these things.* (4:8)

This exhortation by Paul also correlates with Romans 12:1–2 which is a great biblical summary regarding how to live holy lives:

> Therefore I urge you, brethren, by the mercies of God, to present your bodies a living and holy sacrifice, acceptable to God, *which is* your spiritual service of worship. And do not be conformed to this world, but be transformed by the *renewing of your mind,* so that you may prove what the will of God is, that which is good and acceptable and perfect.

A Beautiful Old Testament Example

Richard C. Trench, in his book *Synonyms of the New Testament*, traces the origin of three Greek words, *hagios*, *hosios*, and *hagnos*, which are all translated "holy" or "devout" in the New Testament and used in their various forms approximately 300 times. He then used Joseph as an illustration when he was "tempted to sin by his Egyptian mistress."

- Joseph "approved himself *hosios* in reverencing those everlasting sanctities of the marriage bond, which God had founded, and which he could not violate without sinning against Him."[1] This is the word Paul used when he wrote to Titus in order to describe maturity.
- Joseph "approved himself *hagios* in that he separated himself from any unholy fellowship with his temptress."
- Joseph "approved himself *hagnos* in that he kept his body pure and undefiled."[2]

Note that Joseph lived a holy life in all three dimensions:

- Before the Law was given at Mount Sinai
- Before Jesus Christ came to Earth to model holiness
- Before the Holy Spirit came to indwell and assist mankind in living a holy life
- Before the Word of God was revealed in its entirety

How much more should we as Christians be able to live a holy life today? We have *all* of these resources at our disposal.

Points of Action

This personal project is designed to help you develop the quality of living a more holy life.

Consult the Epistles

To understand holiness and how to live a holy life, we need to look carefully at the letters written to the New Testament churches as well as those letters written to individuals, such as Titus and Timothy, who were responsible for guiding these new and growing bodies of believers.

Check Yourself

As you read, develop a checklist based on exhortations outlined in each New Testament letter. The following is an example from Paul's letter to the Ephesians. These are specific exhortations to live a devout or holy life. As you read through this checklist, evaluate how you measure up to God's expectations. Give yourself a plus symbol (+) where you think you are doing fairly well. Give yourself a check mark (√) where you would like to make some significant improvement.

- ☐ "Laying aside falsehood, speak truth each one of you with his neighbor" (4:25).
- ☐ "Be angry, and yet do not sin; do not let the sun go down on your anger" (v. 26).
- ☐ "He who steals must steal no longer; but rather he must labor, performing with his own hands what is good" (v. 28).
- ☐ "Let no unwholesome word proceed from your mouth, but only such a word as is good for edification" (v. 29).
- ☐ "Do not grieve the Holy Spirit of God" (v. 30).
- ☐ "Let all bitterness and wrath and anger and clamor and slander be put away from you, along with all malice" (v. 31).
- ☐ "Be kind to one another, tenderhearted, forgiving each other" (v. 32).
- ☐ "Walk in love, just as Christ also loved you" (5:2).

☐ "But immorality or any impurity or greed must not even be named among you" (v. 3).

☐ "There must be no filthiness and silly talk, or coarse jesting, which are not fitting, but rather giving of thanks" (v. 4).

☐ "Walk as children of Light (for the fruit of the Light consists in all goodness and righteousness and truth)" (vv. 8–9).

☐ "Do not participate in the unfruitful deeds of darkness, but instead even expose them" (v. 11).

☐ "Be careful how you walk, not as unwise men but as wise, making the most of your time" (vv. 15–16).

☐ "Do not be foolish, but understand what the will of the Lord is" (v. 17).

Personalize Paul's Prayers

Read through Paul's prayers for New Testament Christians and personalize them. You'll notice that most of these prayers focus on living a more holy or devout Christian life. For example, the following is the conclusion of Paul's prayer for the Ephesian Christians. To personalize this prayer, simply insert personal pronouns such as "I," "me," and "my." You can also personalize this prayer for your group by inserting plural pronouns such as "us," "we," and "our."

For this reason I bow my knees before the Father, from whom every family in heaven and on earth derives its name, that He would grant you, according to the riches of His glory, to be *strengthened with power through His Spirit* in the inner man, so *that Christ may dwell in your hearts through faith*; and that you, being rooted and grounded in love, may be able to comprehend with all the saints what is the breadth and length and height and depth, and *to know the love of Christ* which surpasses knowledge, that you may be *filled up to all the fullness of God.* (3:14–19)

Note: You'll find other prayers in Philippians 1:9–11 and Colossians 1:9–12.

Thinking and Growing Together

This section is designed for group discussion and personal application after reading and studying the contents of this chapter:

Suggestions for Discussion and Application

renewal.tv/mm19r

First, make sure someone is appointed to lead the group.

Second, spend time sharing the "greatest learning" from this chapter.

Third, use the following questions for more in-depth discussion.

- What have been your own experiences in clearly understanding what the New Testament teaches about "holiness"?
- Why do most people want to *do* something to make themselves acceptable to God—that is, to be saved?
- Why do people confuse "salvation by grace through faith" with a "works approach" for salvation?
- Would you feel free to share for prayer some of the areas in your life in which you struggle the most in terms of reflecting God's holiness?

Set a Goal

Write out one goal you'd like to achieve as a result of this study.

_____

_____

_____

_____

Pray for One Another

Once each man has written out a goal, allow time to share the goals with others and to pray for each other.

Note: No one in the group should feel forced to share or pray. On the other hand, no one should be excluded from participating.

20

Becoming a Disciplined Man

Self-controlled [disciplined]
Titus 1:8

A 26-Mile Run

When our daughter Robyn was a student at Baylor University, she decided to compete in her first marathon. She launched into a strict training program, running an average of six miles a day and twenty miles every Saturday.

A Personal Message from Gene

renewal.tv/mm20i

During this period of training, I well remember spending a day mountain climbing with her in Montana. I thought I was in fairly good shape physically, until I tried to keep up with her pace. By midafternoon I was in deep trouble. Fortunately, I made it down without having to be carried off the mountain on a stretcher. She was prepared. I wasn't.

Robyn continued this regimen for several months. Frankly, I was rather amazed at her commitment, self-control, and self-discipline. It paid off, because she completed her first race averaging an eight-and-a-half minute mile. What impressed me even more was her physical condition after she had run nonstop for twenty-six miles. Within five minutes, she was breathing normally and experiencing very little muscular discomfort. Because of her strict training program, she was in excellent physical condition. She not only disciplined herself by running, but also in a number of other ways, including her diet.

Temperate, Self-Controlled, Disciplined

As Paul concluded his maturity profile in his letter to Titus, he used the word *egkrate*, which is translated "temperate" in the King James Version, "self-controlled" in the New American Standard Bible, and "disciplined" in the New International Version.

Personally, I prefer the word "disciplined" for two reasons. *First*, this basic concept is used in ancient Greek literature to describe a person who is strong and robust. *Second*, Paul used this word in several athletic illustrations to describe the importance of being disciplined when living the Christian life.

The Greek and Roman Games

Paul was particularly intrigued with athletic analogies. This is understandable. He grew up in Tarsus, a great center for competition. Consequently, he understood Greek and Roman culture, particularly the commitment to develop physical strength and mental concentration in order to engage in vigorous competition in the various Olympic and Isthmian games.

The Isthmian games, second only to the Olympic Games, were held every three years at Corinth. This is apparently why Paul used an athletic metaphor to make a spiritual point in his first letter to the Corinthian Christians. He used a form of *egkrate* in his letter to draw a parallel between living a disciplined Christian life and being a disciplined runner:

> Do you not know that those who *run in a race* all run, but only one receives the prize? Run in such a way that you may win. Everyone who competes in the games exercises *self-control* [self-discipline] in all things. (9:24–25)

In essence, Robyn's story is a modern-day elaboration on the metaphor Paul used in 1 Corinthians to illustrate what it takes to live a victorious Christian life. We cannot reach the goal of becoming mature without being disciplined "in all things." This is why Paul exhorted Timothy, *"Discipline yourself for the purpose of godliness"* (1 Tim. 4:7). Here Paul used the word *gumnazo*, which means to exercise vigorously, either the body or the mind. In athletics, both are involved.

We cannot reach the goal of becoming mature without being disciplined "in all things."

Physical exercise, when it is done properly, is definitely beneficial. It adds to our endurance, and it helps us to be more mentally alert and emotionally stable and resilient. There is evidence that it may add months, and perhaps years, to our lives. But, as Paul reminds us, physical exercise benefits us *only* in this life. On the other hand, maintaining a healthy spiritual life "holds promise for the *present life* and also for the *life to come*" (1 Tim. 4:8).

Spirit and Soul and Body

We are integrated beings. This is why Paul prayed for the Thessalonian Christians that they might be sanctified completely, that their *"spirit* and *soul* and *body* be preserved complete, without blame at the coming of our Lord Jesus Christ" (1 Thess. 5:23).

These three dimensions interrelate in each of our lives. When we are not functioning well *physically*, it affects both our psychological and our spiritual lives. When we are not functioning well *mentally* and *emotionally* (our psychological dimension), it affects our physical and spiritual lives. And when we are out of God's will *spiritually*, it affects us physically and psychologically.

Maintaining Physical and Psychological Health

When you feel depressed and God seems far away, it's important to determine your physical and emotional condition. Are you exercising regularly? Are you getting enough rest? Are you experiencing any chemical imbalances? What about your hormone levels? This is why it is important to get a complete physical examination at least once a year.

I remember a seminary student coming to me one day having serious doubts about the existence of God. Here was a man preparing for the ministry, and yet he was having difficulty believing in the most important truth in Christianity.

After listening to him share his thoughts and feelings, I asked him how much sleep he had been getting. He reported he had been studying night and day trying to unravel and understand some of the mysteries in the Scriptures. At that point, I asked him to eat a good meal and then to go back to his room and go to bed and sleep as long as he could sleep.

Several days later, the same man came back to see me. Guess what? His spiritual doubts were gone, simply because he had overcome his physical and psychological exhaustion. In many respects, he was just like Elijah, who, after his great victory over the prophets of Baal, wanted to die. His thinking became horribly distorted. He was depressed and disillusioned. God's prescription for bringing healing to Elijah was in essence what I suggested to this young student.

God fed Elijah several good meals and then allowed him to sleep. Several days later, Elijah was a different man (see 1 Kings 19:1–8).

Maintaining Spiritual Health

It's also true that as Christians we can experience *many* of the symptoms just mentioned if we're violating God's will. We lose our appetites; we can't sleep well; we are depressed, edgy, and impatient. The problem may be that we're experiencing *real guilt* over our sins, which is affecting both our psychological and physical well-being.

I knew of a Christian man who was committing adultery with a divorced woman. There is no question that he had a sensitive conscience. In his heart, he wanted to be a strong, disciplined Christian, but he knew he was disobeying God. To complicate his guilt, he also knew that he never intended to marry this woman.

The end result of this man's sin was extreme depression—so much so that he couldn't function well at his job. Normally a high-energy person, he lost his desire to achieve. Though he had experienced several other stressful crises in his life, the main cause of his depression seemed to be his sin of living out of God's will for his life. When he acknowledged his sin, claimed God's forgiveness, and refocused his spiritual life, the dark cloud that shrouded his soul disappeared.

Conditioning and Concentration

We don't know who wrote the book of Hebrews, but whoever it was also used the Greek and Roman games to illustrate and describe the disciplines involved in living the Christian life:

> Therefore, since we have so great a cloud of witnesses surrounding us, let us also *lay aside every encumbrance* and the sin which so easily entangles us, and *let us run with endurance the race* that is set before us, *fixing our eyes on Jesus*, the author and perfecter of faith. (12:1–2)

The author of Hebrews broadened this athletic metaphor by using the word *agona*, a Greek athletic term that refers to a contest. Consequently, the author could be referring to a foot race or to other Greek games involving intense competition and self-discipline, such as fighting wild beasts, boxing, wrestling, or throwing the discus.

Lay Aside Every Encumbrance

To compete effectively in these games, an athlete had to "lay aside every encumbrance." He had to "throw off everything that hinders" (NIV). The Greek word is *ogkon*, which refers to "bulk" and "mass." It can refer to excessive weight of any kind, including our own body weight.

Most overweight people have difficulty competing effectively in athletic activities that call for quickness, speed, and endurance. For example, I've spent years skiing. But I learned a rather startling lesson when I allowed myself to put on just ten pounds beyond my normal weight.

I noticed I had trouble breathing, something that hadn't bothered me before. In fact, at extremely high altitudes where I had skied without any difficulties on previous occasions, I thought I was going to hyperventilate. Before, I loved to lead the pack down the mountain, but now I could hardly keep up. Furthermore, my skills had deteriorated. I couldn't trust my abilities.

Then it suddenly dawned on me why I was having so much trouble. I was overweight. To test my theory, I went on a weight-loss program the next month and then went skiing again. The difference was remarkable. I could breathe again. My endurance was back. I could concentrate and stay in control.

Let Us Run with Endurance

The author of Hebrews immediately identified any excessive weight as "the sin which so easily entangles us." Paul called this sin "the deeds of the flesh . . . immorality, impurity, sensuality, idolatry, sorcery, enmities, strife, jealousy, outbursts of anger, disputes, dissensions, factions, envying, drunkenness, carousing, and things like these" (Gal. 5:19–21).

However, what about those weights that aren't so flagrant and noticeable? To be perfectly blunt, are you "ten pounds overweight" in your Christian life? Have you developed habits that keep you from being on the cutting edge spiritually? Are you spending too much time watching television and movies or reading worthless literature? At the same time, are you neglecting your prayer life, church attendance, and Bible reading? To be even more specific, have you developed habits of laziness? Do you lack self-discipline?

Fix Our Eyes on Jesus

"Fixing our eyes on Jesus" is perhaps the most important lesson in this athletic metaphor. Any runner in the Greek stadium who took his eyes off the goal and either looked at the crowds or his competitors would lose valuable time and concentration.

So it is in the Christian life. When we take our eyes off the Lord and focus on others, we are in danger of getting sidetracked spiritually.

> When we take our eyes off the Lord and focus on others, we are in danger of getting sidetracked spiritually.

I remember going through a difficult time in my own life as a young Christian. Several key spiritual leaders I looked up to let me down. They didn't measure up to my expectations. Unfortunately, the experience became disillusioning, so much so that I was tempted to forsake my goal of serving Jesus Christ in full-time ministry. Consequently, I spent a number of months marking time; worse yet, I was losing time.

In retrospect, I learned a valuable lesson. I had taken my eyes off Jesus Christ and focused on others. Unfortunately, these men weren't the best examples in the world. I had to learn that there is only one perfect man—Christ Jesus. He would never let me down. Don't misunderstand. We all need Christians we can look up to as examples. That is why Paul told the Corinthians to imitate him as he imitated Jesus Christ (see 1 Cor. 11:1). Yet we must realize that even the most mature Christians will fail, which is why we must keep our eyes focused on Jesus Christ.

The Homestretch

Paul wrote his last letter while chained in a Roman dungeon. Here, he once again used an athletic metaphor to communicate with Timothy. Paul knew he was coming into the homestretch in his Christian race:

> For I am already being poured out as a drink offering, and the time of my departure has come. (2 Tim. 4:6)

Not too far away from where Paul was incarcerated stood the great Roman Colosseum. Sadly, the Roman games had already deteriorated into a spectator sport that involved fights that pitted men against beasts. The blood-hungry crowds were like animals themselves.

As Paul penned this final letter, he certainly visualized in his mind what was happening in this great arena several blocks away. Using athletic language, he wrote:

> I have fought the good *fight*, I have finished the *course*, I have kept the *faith*; in the future there is laid up for me the *crown of righteousness*, which the Lord, the righteous *Judge*, will *award* to me on that day; and not only to me, but also to all who have loved His appearing. (vv. 7–8)

As Timothy read these words, he would clearly grasp what Paul meant. The word for "fight" (*agonizomai*) conjured up an image of Greek boxers who fought with ox-hide gloves interlaced with lead and iron. The battle itself was brutal, but to fail to win was even more tragic. The loser often had his eyes gouged out.

Paul's final metaphor underscores the seriousness of the Christian life. Our real competitor is Satan. We are in a fight against the forces of evil. Paul had won that fight. He had fought to the finish, and he was about to receive the victor's crown—a special reward for faithfulness and endurance. His faith had not failed him.

Points of Action

In essence, this book entitled *The Measure of a Man* is designed to help each of us as Christian men to "discipline" ourselves "for the purpose of godliness" (1 Tim. 4:7). Paul's two profiles in his letters to Timothy and Titus outline for us nineteen characteristics or qualities that define what this godliness actually is.

Suggestions for Discussion and Application

renewal.tv/mm20r

At the end of each chapter, I have outlined several points of action—steps we can take to develop these particular qualities in our lives. We've also set goals to help us measure up to Christ's stature and fullness (Ephesians 4:13). And now it's time to reflect back to see how we're doing.

Evaluate

In a moment you will be able to review the nineteen characteristics we've studied. A seven-point evaluation scale ranging from *dissatisfaction* to *satisfaction* follows each characteristic. Please read the following directions:

FILL OUT THE QUESTIONNAIRE

Read each question carefully and then circle the number that best represents where you are in your spiritual journey. Be as honest as possible, but give yourself credit where credit is due.

GET ANOTHER POINT OF VIEW

If you are married, have your spouse fill out this questionnaire to reflect her impressions on your attitudes and actions, discuss the questions together, and then compare her scores with your own. If there are discrepancies, discuss why.

Note: If you are single, ask a close male friend to fill out the same survey and follow the same procedures just outlined.

ANALYZE THE RESULTS

First highlight your areas of strength. Then highlight areas where you want to grow and mature and become more disciplined.

REREAD AND REVIEW

Note the areas where you want to improve. Then go back to the chapters in which these qualities are discussed in depth. Reread each chapter and then review the points of action. Once again, set up specific goals you want to achieve in your Christian life.

Determine Your Maturity Quotient

ABOVE REPROACH

1. How do you evaluate your reputation as a Christian among fellow believers as well as among non-Christians?

   1   2   3   4   5   6   7
   Dissatisfied -- Satisfied

THE HUSBAND OF ONE WIFE

2. How do you evaluate your moral life?

   1   2   3   4   5   6   7
   Dissatisfied -- Satisfied

TEMPERATE

3. How do you evaluate the degree to which you are maintaining balance in your Christian experience?

1	2	3	4	5	6	7

Dissatisfied --- Satisfied

PRUDENT

4. How do you evaluate your ability to be wise and discerning?

1	2	3	4	5	6	7

Dissatisfied --- Satisfied

RESPECTABLE

5. How satisfied are you with the way your life reflects the life of Jesus Christ?

1	2	3	4	5	6	7

Dissatisfied --- Satisfied

HOSPITABLE

6. How do you evaluate your use of your material possessions?

1	2	3	4	5	6	7

Dissatisfied --- Satisfied

ABLE TO TEACH

7. How do you evaluate your ability to communicate with others who may disagree with you?

1	2	3	4	5	6	7

Dissatisfied --- Satisfied

NOT ADDICTED TO WINE

8. To what degree are you satisfied with your ability to control various kinds of obsessions and compulsions?

1	2	3	4	5	6	7

Dissatisfied -- Satisfied

NOT SELF-WILLED

9. How satisfied are you with your ability to relate to other people without being self-centered and controlling?

1	2	3	4	5	6	7

Dissatisfied -- Satisfied

NOT QUICK-TEMPERED

10. How satisfied are you with the way you handle anger?

1	2	3	4	5	6	7

Dissatisfied -- Satisfied

NOT PUGNACIOUS

11. How satisfied are you with your ability to control any form of verbal or physical abuse?

1	2	3	4	5	6	7

Dissatisfied -- Satisfied

GENTLE

12. How objective and fair-minded are you in your relationships with others?

1	2	3	4	5	6	7

Dissatisfied -- Satisfied

PEACEABLE (UNCONTENTIOUS)

13. How satisfied are you with your ability to avoid arguments?

1	2	3	4	5	6	7

Dissatisfied --- Satisfied

FREE FROM THE LOVE OF MONEY

14. How satisfied are you with your ability to be nonmaterialistic?

1	2	3	4	5	6	7

Dissatisfied --- Satisfied

MANAGES HIS OWN HOUSEHOLD WELL

15. If you are a father, how satisfied are you with your ability to function in this role according to God's plan?

1	2	3	4	5	6	7

Dissatisfied --- Satisfied

LOVING WHAT IS GOOD

16. To what degree are you satisfied with your efforts at overcoming evil with good?

1	2	3	4	5	6	7

Dissatisfied --- Satisfied

JUST

17. How satisfied are you with your ability to be just and fair in your relationships with others?

1	2	3	4	5	6	7

Dissatisfied --- Satisfied

DEVOUT (HOLY)

18. To what degree are you satisfied with the way your life reflects God's holiness?

| 1 | 2 | 3 | 4 | 5 | 6 | 7 |

Dissatisfied --- Satisfied

SELF-CONTROLLED (DISCIPLINED)

19. How satisfied are you with your ability to live a disciplined Christian life?

| 1 | 2 | 3 | 4 | 5 | 6 | 7 |

Dissatisfied --- Satisfied

A Final Word

The profile we've looked at in this study is definitely outlined for men. It's a profile of Christ-like maturity. This is clear in Paul's statement that a mature man is morally pure—loyal to only one woman in his life—his wife. Later he stated that a mature man is a good father who leads his family well.

Biblical profiles exist for other people, as well; for a profile outlined specifically for women, see the book I wrote with my wife, Elaine, titled *The Measure of a Woman*. You can also find *The Measure of a Young Man*, which I authored with my son, Kenton.

The fact is, most of the qualities we've looked at in this study are repeated elsewhere in Scripture for all Christ-followers. In this sense, the qualities Paul outlined in 1 Timothy 3 and Titus 1 are specific goals to aim for as we practice what he challenged the Roman Christians to do when he wrote:

> I beseech you therefore, brethren, by the mercies of God, to present your bodies a living sacrifice, holy, acceptable to God, which is your spiritual service. And be not fashioned according to this world: but be ye transformed by the renewing of your mind, that ye may prove what is the good and acceptable and perfect will of God. (Rom. 12:1–2 ASV)

Notes

Chapter 7 Sharing Our Resources

1. "Peace Prayer of St. Francis of Assisi," Catholic News Agency, http://www.catholicnewsagency.com/resources/saints/saints/peace-prayer-of-st-francis-of-assisi/.
2. Henry Drummond, *Addresses* (Philadelphia: Henry Altemus, 1892), 27–28.

Chapter 9 Being Moderate in All Things

1. Merrill F. Unger, *Unger's Bible Dictionary* (Chicago: Moody Press, 1967), 1168.
2. *Children of Alcoholics: Important Facts* (Rockville, MD: National Association for Children of Alcoholics), 2.
3. "Health Effects of Smoking," American Lung Association, n.d. http://www.lung.org/stop-smoking/smoking-facts/health-effects-of-smoking.html.
4. "Tobacco Use and Pregnancy," Centers for Disease Control and Prevention, September 9, 2015. http://www.cdc.gov/reproductivehealth/maternalinfanthealth/tobaccousepregnancy/.
5. "Health Effects of Smoking," American Lung Association, n.d. http://www.lung.org/stop-smoking/smoking-facts/health-effects-of-smoking.html.
6. "Vital Signs: Tobacco Use," Centers for Disease Control and Prevention, September 2010. http://www.cdc.gov/vitalsigns/TobaccoUse/Smoking/index.html.
7. "Health Effects of Smoking," American Lung Association, n.d. http://www.lung.org/stop-smoking/smoking-facts/health-effects-of-smoking.html.

Chapter 10 Overcoming Self-Centeredness

1. Joseph H. Thayer, *Greek-English Lexicon of the New Testament* (Grand Rapids: Zondervan Publishing House, 1962), 83.
2. *The Holy Bible in the Language of Today: An American Translation*, trans. William F. Beck (Philadelphia: A. J. Holman Company, 1976), n.p.
3. *The New Testament in the Language of the People*, trans. Charles B. Williams (Chicago: Moody Press, 1937), n.p.

Chapter 12 Avoiding Destructive Behavior

1. Joseph H. Thayer, *Greek-English Lexicon of the New Testament* (Grand Rapids: Zondervan Publishing House, 1962), 516.
2. Chuck Colson, "The Terrifying Truth: We Are Normal," *Jubilee* (July 1983), n.p.
3. Robert L. Vernon, *L. A. Justice* (Colorado Springs: Focus on the Family Publishing, 1993), 190–91.
4. "What Is Domestic Violence?," National Coalition against Domestic Violence, accessed October 1, 2015. http://www.ncadv.org/need-help/what-is-domestic-violence.
5. "National Statistics," National Coalition against Domestic Violence, accessed March 17, 2016. http://ncadv.org/learn/statistics.

Chapter 13 Treating Others Fairly

1. Bob St. John, *The Landry Legend* (Dallas, TX: WORD Inc., 1989), 283.
2. Ibid., 156.
3. Ibid., 291.
4. Ibid., 157.
5. Ibid., 23.
6. Ibid., 286.
7. Joseph H. Thayer, *Greek-English Lexicon of the New Testament* (Grand Rapids, MI: Zondervan Publishing House, 1962), 238.
8. St. John, *The Landry Legend,* 157.
9. Ibid.
10. Ibid., 154.

Chapter 15 Learning Generosity

1. Results of the study are now published in the book *Rich in Every Way* (n.p.: Howard Publishers, 2004).

Chapter 17 Loving God Wholeheartedly

1. Paul Lee Tan, *Encyclopedia of 7,700 Illustrations* (Rockville, MD: Assurance Publishers, 1979), 830.

Chapter 18 Being Just and Upright

1. Martin Luther, *Luther's Works,* vol. 54, ed. Weimar (n.p.), 179.
2. Ibid.

Chapter 19 Living a Holy Life

1. Richard C. Trench, *Synonyms of the New Testament* (Grand Rapids, MI: William B. Eerdmans Publishing Co., 1948), 333–34.
2. Ibid.

Gene A. Getz is pastor emeritus at Chase Oaks Church in Plano, Texas, and director of the Center for Church Renewal. He is the author of more than sixty books and has authored the *Life Essentials Study Bible* which contains 1,500 "Principles to Live By." He has taught at Moody Bible Institute and Dallas Theological Seminary. In 1972 he started the first Fellowship Bible Church in Dallas, TX, which has now multiplied to hundreds of Fellowship churches. To access Gene's daily Bible principles that are aired daily on numerous radio stations, go to www.bibleprinciples.org. You can also access the resources by downloading a free app entitled Life Essentials QR Reader. Gene has been married to his wife, Elaine, for over sixty years. He has three children and eight grandchildren.

Bible Principles.org
Home of the Life Essentials Study Bible | By Gene Getz

Dr. Gene Getz's primary focus is to reach audiences around the world with the Word of God. BiblePrinciples.org is a forum for free Bible teaching and ministry.

- Watch Gene's 42 teaching videos that accompany *The Measure of a Man*

- Use the Principle Finder to access Gene's 1,500 "Principles to Live By" videos in discussing 241 topics found from Genesis to Revelation

- Listen to Gene's daily two-minute radio feature entitled "Bible Principles"

- Access The Center for Church Renewal online bookstore where you can order the *Life Essentials Study Bible* and Gene's numerous books

- Read relevant and engaging articles by Gene

- Sign up for Gene's newsletter and notifications on special live streaming events

Visit www.BiblePrinciples.org today!

Discover God's Definition
of True Beauty

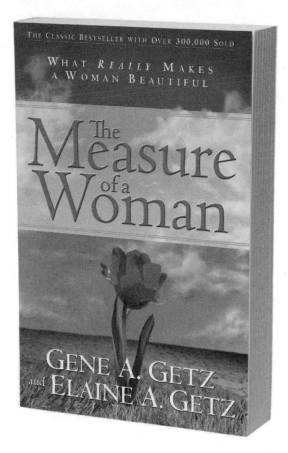

Revell
a division of Baker Publishing Group
www.RevellBooks.com

Available wherever books and ebooks are sold.

——— Seven Keys to Becoming ———

A MAN OF FAITH, STRENGTH, AND GODLY CHARACTER

"As another father-and-son team, we highly recommend this book."
Josh McDowell & Sean McDowell

THE MEASURE OF A YOUNG MAN

Become the Man God Wants You to Be

Gene A. Getz
Bestselling Author of *The Measure of a Man*
Kenton Getz

Revell
a division of Baker Publishing Group
www.RevellBooks.com

Available wherever books and ebooks are sold.

Be the First to Hear about Other New Books from REVELL!

Sign up for announcements about new and upcoming titles at

RevellBooks.com/SignUp

Don't miss out on our great reads!

Revell

a division of Baker Publishing Group
www.RevellBooks.com